THE BENTO LUNCHBOX

Sachiko Horie

TUTTLE Publishing

Tokyo | Rutland, Vermont | Singapore

Contents

Part 1
Main Dishes
My Approach to Mains 38

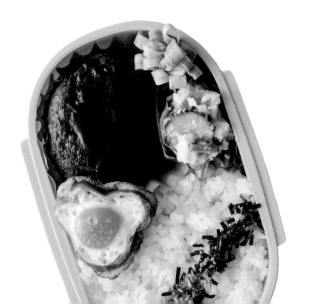

Part 2

Side Dishes

My Approach to Sides 72

Part 3
Rice, Noodles & Bread

My Approach to Starches 106

Master the Basics With this Definitive Guide to Japanese Bentos

Thank you for choosing this book from among the many bento cookbooks out there! If you want to master the Japanese art of tasty, healthy homemade lunches, you've come to the right place.

My style of bento cooking doesn't require any difficult techniques or unfamiliar seasonings, and my recipes work for both adults and children. I hope they'll soon become lunchbox staples for you—and maybe even join the menu for your everyday meals at home. Great recipes are the heart of this book. But I also explain the basics of bento making that are unfamiliar to many people (even in Japan!). Plenty of step-by-step photos make the instructions easier for beginning cooks to understand. I've also included lots of tips for making food tastier and the cook's job easier that I've discovered during my own bento-making journey.

We all worry about what to make for lunch every day, right?

On busy days, I plop one item on top of rice and call it done. On hot days, I pack cold noodles; on cold days, I bring hot soup in a thermos; and on days when I can't shop, I pull out prepped items from the freezer. I stir up seasonings the night before and gather ingredients in a container to have on standby in the fridge.

I hope the time you spend preparing lunch becomes a fun part of each day. And I hope this book brings happiness to both the cook and the eaters!

—Sachiko Horie

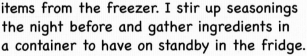

How to Use This Book

The book is divided into four parts: an introductory section explaining the basics of bento cooking plus three sections with simple recipes for mains, sides and starches. Here's a quick guide to using the book.

Introduction

Bento basics plus six Master Bentos to guide your menu planning

This is where you'll find the basic information you need to get started, divided into six categories. Then I show you how to put together six Master Bentos for different kinds of eaters.

Model bentos for each type of eater

Photos show the color and nutritional balance of each bento type at a glance.

Bento box volume and amount of rice

A guide to bento box size and amount of rice for each type of bento.

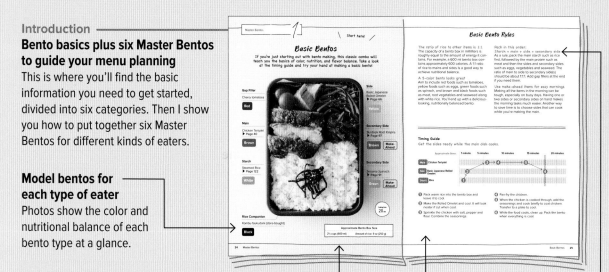

Efficient bento prep schedule

Follow these detailed steps to make a single bento in 15 to 20 minutes.

Tips for each bento type

Key points to guarantee success.

Part 1

Mains organized by ingredient

This section has recipes for the "main dish" of the bento. Organized by protein type such as chicken, pork, beef and seafood so you can use what you have on hand.

Calories and estimated cooking time

All recipes in the three main sections include calorie information and estimated cooking time to help you stay healthy and make the most of your busy mornings.

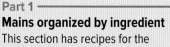

Shelf life

Knowing how long make-ahead recipes stay fresh lets you plan ahead by doubling or tripling the quantity for use in multiple bentos.

Step-by-step photos

Photos highlight key techniques that ensure even beginners get great results.

Recipe variations

Easy variations using different ingredients or seasonings.

Part 2

Sides organized by color

Healthy side dishes boost the vitamin and mineral content of your bentos. The recipes are organized by color (red, yellow, green, brown, black and white) so balancing color is easy.

"Quick" and "Make Ahead" sections

Quick sides use just a few ingredients and are done in about 5 minutes. Make-ahead sides are ready to pack straight from the fridge.

Part 3

Starches

Rice, bread and noodles star in the bentos featured in this section. You'll find lots of ideas for easy one-dish lunches packed with vegetables and protein.

Lots of variations!

From thermos bentos to rice balls, sandwiches, pasta and more, variations expand your bento repertoire in a snap.

Detailed instructions for cooking and packing

With photos and tips for food safety, packing your bento attractively, and keeping it tasty even after the food has cooled.

About the Recipe Notations

Quantities are for easy-to-prepare portions with minimum waste. Serving size is for adults 18 to 60 years of age with normal physical activity levels. When cooking for children, adjust quantities according to the size of the lunch box; for example, halve the ingredient quantities.

1 tablespoon = 15 ml, 1 teaspoon = 5 ml, and 1 cup = 240 ml. "A little" indicates less than ⅙ teaspoon.

Microwave oven times use 600 watt ovens as the standard. If using a higher wattage oven, reduce the cooking times. Test for doneness and add time as needed.

Wash and peel vegetables before using, unless otherwise noted.

Allow make-ahead items to cool fully before storing.

Transfer to a clean container with clean utensils.

Shelf life is only a guide and may vary depending on cold air circulation in the refrigerator or freezer and how often you open the door; try to use items as soon as possible.

Calorie counts are for one serving. If a recipe serves 1 to 2, calories are for ½ the recipe. If the recipe serves 3 to 4, calories are for ¼ the recipe. For items such as hard boiled eggs or meatballs, calories are given per piece. The amount of food eaten will vary depending on age, gender, body type, appetite, and other factors, so please use the calorie counts only as a general guide.

Cooking time indicates the time required for active cooking, excluding marinating, cooling, and similar steps.

Know Your Tools

Let's start with the equipment needed to make bento lunchboxes, such as bento boxes, cooking utensils and divider cups. Read on to learn about easy-to-use sizes, materials and varieties.

The Size of the Bento Box

It's important to choose the right size bento box for the person who will be using it.

For Small Children
1 to 1⅔ cup (250–400 ml) capacity

For small children aged 3 to 5 years, choose a bento box that holds 1 cup to 1⅔ cups (250–400 ml). If they are not used to eating from a bento box or have a small appetite, use a box on the smaller side. The size should match the child's appetite.

For Women
2 to 3⅓ cup (500–800 ml) capacity

Women between the age of 18 and 60 will typically need a bento box that holds 2 to 2½ cups (500–600 ml). Growing middle and high school girls may need a 3 cup (700 ml) bento box depending on their appetite, and girls who play sports may need a 3⅓ cup (800 ml) box.

For Men
3 to 4 cup (700–1000 ml) capacity

A typical adult male will need a box that holds around 3¾ cups (900 ml), depending on activity level. For boys in middle and high school, a 3 to 3⅓ cup (700–800 ml) bento box is recommended, since they typically snack in addition to their lunch. For boys who play sports, a capacity of 3⅓ to 4 cups (800–1000 ml) is recommended.

Types of Bento Boxes

Bento boxes come in various materials, each with its own pluses, minuses and care guidelines.

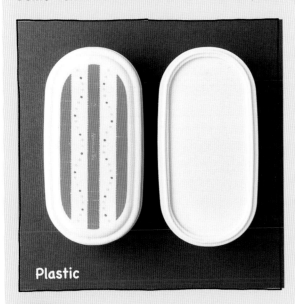

Plastic

Pluses Many colors, designs and shapes. Okay for microwave or dishwasher.

Minuses Easily absorb colors and odors. Short lifespan.

Care Wash by hand with dish soap, or in the dishwasher. Use kitchen bleach for stains and odors.

Aluminum

Pluses Lightweight, heat up fast in a warmer. Shallow ones are good for kids.

Minuses Can't be put in the microwave or dishwasher. Leak easily.

Care Alkaline detergents turn aluminum black. Use neutral dish soap.

Bentwood

Pluses Beautiful and fragrant. Wick away excess moisture to keep food tasting great.

Minuses Not airtight. Can't be put in the microwave or dishwasher.

Care Wash as soon as it is used and let dry completely to avoid discoloration.

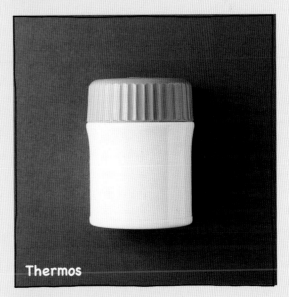

Thermos

Pluses Essential for packing liquids. Great heat and cold retention, airtight.

Minuses Heavy. Can't be put in the microwave or dishwasher.

Care Remove inner and outer lid and seal before washing. After washing, carefully wipe and let air-dry completely.

Cooking Utensils

These are the basic cooking utensils you'll need to prepare the recipes in this book.

Large, medium and small heatproof bowls

A small skillet

Choose heatproof, microwave-safe bowls so you can use them for cooking as well as mixing and flavoring ingredients. It's convenient to have various sizes for different uses.

I recommend using a skillet that's not too big for the amount of food you're cooking. For bentos, you will often be making a small amount of food, so it's best to use a pan with a 7- or 8-inch (18–20 cm) diameter. If it's on the deep side, you can use it for boiling and shallow frying, too.

Square omelet pan

Measuring spoons, small cutting board and kitchen knife

I recommend a square pan if you plan to make rolled omelets often. They can be used for other foods, too, such as boiled vegetables or stir-fries. Choose one with a non-stick coating.

Small cutting boards are easy to wash and convenient for cutting soft foods. I recommend having both a small knife and a standard-sized one for different tasks. You'll also need a set of measuring spoons for seasonings.

Convenient Items for Packing a Bento Box

Having these items on hand will help you make great-looking bentos.

Wax Paper

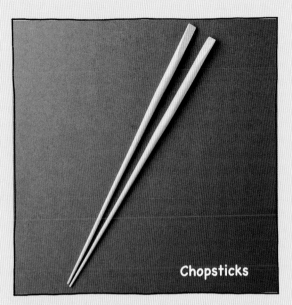

Chopsticks

Use this water-resistant paper to divide or wrap food. Wax paper keeps your bento box clean when packing teriyaki or deep-fried items. It's also great for wrapping sandwiches. Fun patterned wax paper is available for purchase online.

Chopsticks are very useful for arranging food. A special variety made just for this purpose has thin, pointed tips for easily grabbing small bits of food—but any pair of chopsticks will do.

Food Cups

Food Picks

Choose easy-to-use materials and sizes. Paper and aluminum cups can be squeezed into any space, while silicone cups can be washed and reused. Food cups come in round, square and other shapes, and in different depths—choose those that fit your box.

Food picks boost the cuteness factor and make sides easier to eat. They come in different lengths; some are just right for one cherry tomato, while others can hold two or three items at once. Check specialty or online shops to find them.

Step 2
Keep these foods on hand!

Know Your Ingredients

Having certain ingredients in your pantry, fridge and freezer makes bento prep a lot easier. Below you'll find foods to always have in the fridge, easy toppings for rice, useful dried foods and frozen vegetables, and handy seasonings. For information on the Japanese ingredients used in this book, see page 140.

Refrigerator Must-Haves

Ham
Cherry tomatoes
Sliced cheese
Smoked sausages
Eggs
Processed cheese
Shredded pizza cheese

Toppings to Liven Up Rice

Furikake topping
Tsukudani preserves
Salted kombu
Pickled plums
Pickled vegetables

Keep a variety of versatile ingredients in the fridge.
Pictured are a few ingredients to always keep in the fridge. Eggs can be used in omelets or added to stir-fried vegetables. Processed meats such as sausage and ham can go into stir-fries and salads. Keep several kinds of cheese on hand for a variety of dishes.

Add color and flavor to steamed rice.
Plain steamed rice often takes up about half of a bento box. Adding a "rice companion" such as salty tsukudani preserves, pickled plums, furikake topping, salted kombu, or pickles boost color and flavor. Pickled plums also have a sterilizing effect that helps prevent spoilage.

Dried Foods that Make Easy Sides

Bonito flakes Dried daikon radish

Hijiki seaweed Glass noodles

Dried goods are useful for make-ahead items and to mix with other foods.
Classic Japanese dried goods like shredded daikon and hijiki seaweed keep well at room temperature and can be cooked in the microwave, so they're great to have in the pantry. Bonito flakes instantly turn vegetables into a yummy side.

Frozen Vegetables to Add Color

Frozen green beans

Frozen edamame

Frozen vegetables can be a lifesaver. Keep several types on hand.
Keep some vegetables in the freezer to add an easy pop of color to your bento. Simply defrost edamame, sprinkle lightly with salt and add to your lunch. Frozen kabocha squash and broccoli are also convenient.

Essential Seasonings

Sake Soy sauce Salt

Mirin Vinegar Sugar

Miso Black pepper

These are your simple, go-to seasonings.
The basic bento seasonings are sugar, salt, vinegar, soy sauce and miso. Add sake, mirin and black pepper, and you can make almost all standard Japanese dishes.

Seasonings That Are Nice To Have

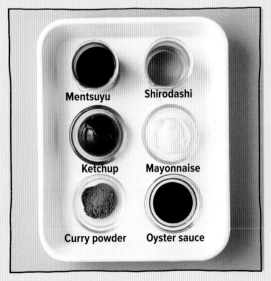

Mentsuyu Shirodashi

Ketchup Mayonnaise

Curry powder Oyster sauce

Use these to vary flavors and please the kids.
Ketchup and mayo are popular with kids. Mentsuyu and shirodashi can be used on their own. Curry powder and oyster sauce add a different taste.

Step 3

Color, taste and nutrition

Plan Your Menu

Now that you know what equipment and ingredients you'll need, it's time to think about menu planning. Focusing on the following three points will help you create a bento that satisfies the eyes, body and taste buds.

Key Elements and Color

A basic Japanese bento box contains one main starch, one main protein and two sides. If space is left or you want a burst of color, add a gap filler. Using five colors helps make a bento look delicious the moment you open the lid.

Main Protein

A dish featuring meat, fish or another protein. Increase your repertoire to include grilling, stir-frying, deep-frying and more.

Main Starch

The main carbohydrate, such as rice, noodles or bread. For a change from plain steamed rice, try cooking meat or vegetables with the rice or folding them in after it's cooked.

Rice Companion

Topping white rice with a "companion" such as sesame seeds, furikake, or pickles adds color and flavor.

Side Dish

Rolled omelets are a classic bento side dish. For a sampling of the many variations on rolled omelets, see page 68.

Secondary Side Dish

The second side dish usually features vegetables, seaweed or mushrooms. Having a few salads or stewed dishes ready for this purpose is convenient.

Gap Filler

Adding colorful fillers is the last step in packing a bento. Cherry tomatoes and boiled vegetables are easy and convenient fillers.

Nutritional Balance

Health is as important as color and flavor in a bento. Including a starch, a main, and two sides naturally provides nutritional balance.

Starch
Carbohydrates

Main
Protein

Side
Vitamins and Minerals

Rice, noodles, bread
Carbohydrate-rich foods contain the energy we need for an active lifestyle. Pack half the bento box with the main starch.

Meat, seafood, tofu
Proteins like meat and seafood not only provide energy, they also keep skin healthy and are the building blocks for muscles and organs.

Eggs, vegetables, seaweed
Eggs contain almost all nutrients other than vitamin C and fiber. Vegetables, seaweed and mushrooms are loaded with vitamins and minerals.

Flavor

When planning a bento, it's important not to repeat the same flavors. A salty main should be paired with a sweet side and a sour secondary side, for instance. Combine four different flavors for a well-balanced bento.

Salty

Sweet

Sour

Hot and Spicy

Salt, miso, soy sauce
A central flavor in standard Japanese dishes such as stir-fries, grilled dishes, and dressed vegetables.

Sugar, mirin, honey
Many Japanese mains and sides are sweet, including nimono (simmered vegetables or meat), teriyaki, and some pickles and preserves, like tsukudani.

Vinegar, lemon
Lemon, wine vinegar, mayonnaise and ponzu sauce can all create sour flavors. Sweet-and-sour dishes belong in this category, too.

Spices, chili pepper
Black pepper, curry powder, doubanjiang (Chinese spicy bean paste) and chili peppers all add a kick to your bento.

Prepping and Cooking

Step 4
Put it all together fast

On the next four pages, you'll find tips for prepping the day before and shortening cooking time that will help you make bentos more efficiently in the morning. And don't forget to follow the food safety tips!

Prepare the Day Before

Getting ready the day before makes your morning bento routine much easier.

Gather and prep ingredients ahead of time

If you are a bento beginner, plan your menu the day before and put all the necessary ingredients in a shallow tray or similar container in the refrigerator. Things will go more smoothly the next morning! Cut and measure everything so all that's left is cooking and seasoning.

TIP
Make some dishes in advance
Does cooking everything in the morning feel overwhelming? Try preparing at least one make-ahead item that can be cooked in a big batch and stored, so you can simply pack it into your bento box in the morning. It's even better to have several vegetable and seaweed sides in a variety of colors on hand.

Marinate
Pre-season meat and seafood
Start marinating the meat for dishes like Karaage Fried Chicken the day before to improve both efficiency and flavor. Sprinkle fish with salt so it doesn't smell fishy.

Cut up vegetables
Ready to cook with zero stress
Cutting up all the vegetables you'll need the day before saves time in the morning since you can start cooking right away. I recommend boiling vegetables like broccoli and carrots the day before, too.

Combine seasonings
Mix ingredients in small bowls
For dishes flavored with several seasonings after cooking, it's a good idea to measure out and combine the seasonings the day before. Adding them in the morning is a snap.

TIP

Get creative with using dinner for lunch
If you make fried chicken or hamburger steaks for dinner, freeze some of the prepped meat for a bento several days later. Freeze curry in one-meal portions. If you plan to use dinner in the next day's bento, shake things up by changing the sauce, topping stew with melted cheese, or other tweaks.

Cook Several Items at the Same Time

Shorten cooking time by using a skillet, toaster oven, microwave and rice cooker.

Cook two items in a skillet at once
Save time by cooking small items together in a skillet. For example, you can fry eggs or stir-fry vegetables while you pan-fry sausages.

Bake two items in a toaster oven at once
When cooking meat or fish mains in a toaster oven, you can save time by nestling vegetables or mushrooms next to them for a side.

Use the Microwave and Skillet at the Same Time

Once you've prepped all the ingredients for your bento, cook one dish in the microwave and another in the skillet. Using a rice cooker is another effortless way to save time; you can preset it at night to have rice ready to go in the morning.

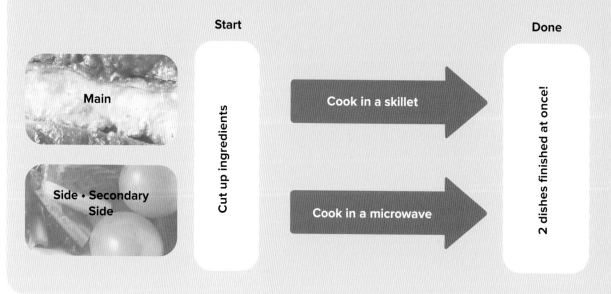

Start

Done

Main

Cut up ingredients

Cook in a skillet

Side • Secondary Side

Cook in a microwave

2 dishes finished at once!

Pay Attention to Food Safety

Bentos spend a lot of time at room temperature, so don't forget to take food safety seriously, especially on hot or humid days. Let's review a few key points.

Add flour to thicken liquids
Bacteria flourish in moist environments, so sprinkle some flour onto stir-fries and other dishes to reduce moisture.

Cook thoroughly
Cooking foods through to the center helps kill bacteria. Check to be sure food is thoroughly cooked by cutting into the center of one piece.

Season food well
Bacteria tends not to grow well in well-seasoned foods, so they spoil less easily. Well-seasoned food also tastes better when cold.

Use ingredients with antimicrobial properties
Make smart use of ingredients that ward off bad bacteria, such as pickled plums, green shiso leaves, vinegar and curry powder.

Drain off liquid before packing
To prevent bacteria from multiplying, put very moist items on a plate lined with paper towels to absorb liquid.

Pack make-ahead items with clean utensils
When packing make-ahead items into a bento, be sure to use clean utensils so you don't contaminate the portion you put in the bento or what goes back in the fridge.

Extra points for making it pretty!

Pack it Up

Once everything is cooked, it's time to pack the bento box. Follow the steps shown in the pictures below. Make sure you pay attention to the shape of the bento box, as it will affect the way it's filled.

How to Pack a Rectangular Bento Box

Start!

Once you've packed the rice, let it cool.

1

Fill half the box with warm rice.

Lining the other half makes clean-up easier.

2

Line the other half with wax paper.

Pack the food against the corners of the box.

5

Pack the rolled omelet with its tidy cut sides up in the back cup.

For the front cup, use foods that can be molded to any shape.

6

Pack the secondary side in the front cup and add gap fillers.

How to Pack Boxes with Other Shapes

Round bento box
Pack rice into about half the bento box, making a sloped border between the rice and the other food. Lean the other foods against the rice.

Oval bento box
A ring of furikake along the edge of the rice looks cute.

Two-tier bento box
Fill one tier with cylindrical rice balls and line up food cups for the main and sides in the other tier.

Decide where you want the sides to go.

3

Place the cups for the side and secondary side on the right.

The key is to leave as few gaps as possible.

4

Pack the main on the left.

7

The rice companion makes plain rice look good!

Add a rice companion such as black sesame seeds.

Ready to go!

Step 6

Reduce waste without sacrificing taste!

Making Items Ahead

Fully prepared refrigerated and frozen items are key for easy morning prep. Follow these tips for freezing and thawing food so it tastes as good as fresh.

Use the Right Storage Containers

Start by choosing the right types of container for refrigerator and freezer storage.

Use large containers, food cups and bags.

Use freezer bags to pre-flavor ingredients in the freezer
Frozen items should not be exposed to air, so I recommend putting them in freezer bags and pressing out all the air before sealing.

Food cups are convenient for storing sides in single servings
If you store side dishes in silicon cups, you can pack them into your bento cup and all. Silicon cups work for the refrigerator and the freezer.

Store mains in plastic containers
Store pan-fried or stir-fried mains in large plastic containers. Stewed and marinated dishes can also be stored successfully in these containers.

Tips For Refrigerator Storage

Follow these important rules to ensure your food keeps well in the fridge.

Spray storage containers with alcohol
Use clean, completely dry containers to store food. To be extra safe, spray storage containers with alcohol before putting food in them.

Cool food completely before refrigerating
Food should be completely cool before transferring to storage containers and covering. Otherwise, condensation will develop on the lid, increasing the likelihood of spoilage. Eat whatever you store within 3 to 5 days.

Tips For Freezer Storage

Here's how to store food in the freezer and defrost it without losing taste or texture.

Wrap in cling film and seal to prevent exposure to air
The key to successful freezer storage is to prevent food from being exposed to air. Wrap items individually in cling film, put in a freezer bag, and press out as much air as you can before sealing.

Defrost food in a heatproof bowl in the microwave
Place frozen food in a heatproof bowl, cover loosely with cling film and heat in the microwave. Cool and pack into the bento box. Pre-seasoned ingredients can be defrosted under cold running water or at room temperature.

1

Start here!

Basic Bentos

If you're just starting out with bento making, this classic combo will teach you the basics of color, nutrition, and flavor balance. Take a look at the timing guide and try your hand at making a basic bento!

Gap Filler

Cherry tomatoes

 Red

Main

Chicken Teriyaki
▶ Page 40

Brown

Starch

Steamed Rice
▶ Page 122

White

Rice Companion

Kombu tsukudani (store-bought)

Black

Side

Basic Japanese
Rolled Omelet
▶ Page 66

Yellow

Secondary Side

Burdock Root Kinpira
▶ Page 97

Brown | Make-Ahead

Secondary Side

Sesame Spinach
▶ Page 91

Green | Make-Ahead

Cooking time
20 min

Approximate Bento Box Size	
2½ cups (600 ml)	Amount of rice: 9 oz (250 g)

Basic Bento Rules

The ratio of rice to other items is 1:1
The capacity of a bento box in milliliters is roughly equal to the amount of energy it contains. For example, a 600 ml bento box contains approximately 600 calories. A 1:1 ratio of rice to mains and sides is a good way to achieve nutritional balance.

A 5-color bento looks great
Aim to include red foods such as tomatoes, yellow foods such as eggs, green foods such as spinach, and brown and black foods such as meat, root vegetables and seaweed along with white rice. You'll end up with a delicious-looking, nutritionally balanced bento.

Pack in this order:
Starch + main + side + secondary side
As a rule, pack the main starch such as rice first, followed by the main protein such as meat and then the sides and secondary sides such as eggs, vegetables and seaweed. The ratio of main to side to secondary side(s) should be about 1:1:1. Add gap fillers at the end if you need them.

Use make-ahead items for easy mornings
Making all the items in the morning can be tough, especially on busy days. Having one or two sides or secondary sides on hand makes the morning tasks much easier. Another way to save time is to choose sides that can cook while you're making the main.

Timing Guide
Get the sides ready while the main dish cooks.

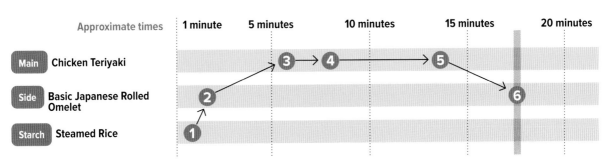

1. Pack warm rice into the bento box and leave it to cool.
2. Make the Rolled Omelet and cool. It will look neater if cut when cool.
3. Sprinkle the chicken with salt, pepper and flour. Combine the seasonings.
4. Pan-fry the chicken.
5. When the chicken is cooked through, add the seasonings and cook briefly to coat chicken. Transfer to a plate to cool.
6. While the food cools, clean up. Pack the bento when everything is cool.

\ **For hard-working dads...
and others with high
calorie needs** /

Hearty Bentos

For men who do physical work or sports, as well as
others with an active lifestyle and high calorie needs, pack a hearty,
satisfying bento. Don't forget to provide balanced nutrition, too.

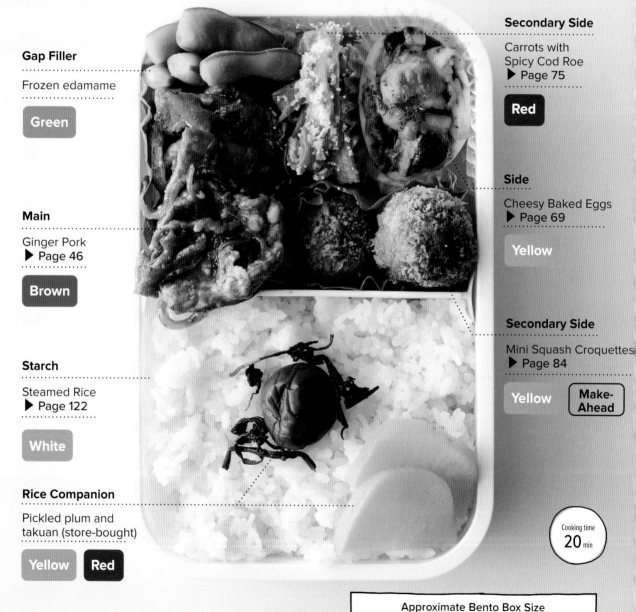

Gap Filler

Frozen edamame

`Green`

Main

Ginger Pork
▶ Page 46

`Brown`

Starch

Steamed Rice
▶ Page 122

`White`

Rice Companion

Pickled plum and
takuan (store-bought)

`Yellow` `Red`

Secondary Side

Carrots with
Spicy Cod Roe
▶ Page 75

`Red`

Side

Cheesy Baked Eggs
▶ Page 69

`Yellow`

Secondary Side

Mini Squash Croquettes
▶ Page 84

`Yellow` `Make-Ahead`

Cooking time
20 min

Approximate Bento Box Size	
4 cups (1000 ml)	Amount of rice: 10½ oz (300 g)

Hearty Bento Rules

Pack plenty of rice and other dishes

Use a large bento box that holds 4 cups (900 to 1000 ml). The key is to maintain the 1:1 ratio of rice to other dishes while packing plenty of each. Choose recipes that are hearty and well seasoned to increase satiety.

Don't worry too much about color balance

When heartiness is the main goal, you don't have to obsess about color balance. Once you've packed the eater's favorite foods, supplement with frozen edamame, pickled plums, yellow pickled daikon, and other colorful accents.

Pack favorite foods but pay attention to nutrition

Even though satisfaction is the priority, packing only favorite foods can skew the nutritional balance. For instance, if you pack a filling meat dish, add a vegetable side such as carrots or kabocha squash to keep it well balanced.

TIP: Pasta can be a side

For people who need lots of energy, pack plenty of carbs. In addition to rice, you can achieve this by adding noodles or pasta salad, kabocha squash, potatoes, glass noodles, or similar items.

Timing Guide

Warm up the make-ahead Mini Squash Croquettes in the toaster oven with the Cheesy Baked Eggs.

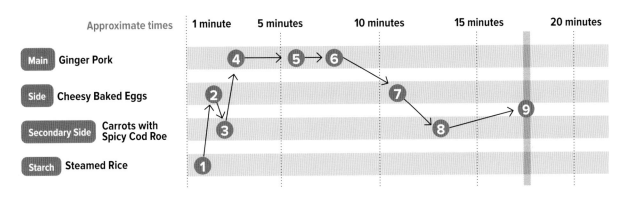

1. Pack warm rice into the bento box and leave it to cool.
2. Start boiling the egg.
3. Cut up the carrot for the secondary side.
4. Cut up the onion for the main.
5. Cut the pork for the main and sprinkle with salt and pepper. Combine the seasonings for the pork.
6. Pan-fry the pork.
7. Bake the Cheesy Baked Eggs in the toaster oven. Warm the defrosted Mini Squash Croquettes next to it.
8. While the egg and croquettes cook, make the Carrots with Spicy Cod Roe.
9. While the food cools, clean up. Pack the bento when everything is cool.

\ For people watching their weight /

Healthy Bentos

This bento is ideal for people with low calorie needs or those on a diet. Although I have used white rice here, I also recommend rice with mixed grains. Several companies sell a mix of seven or more grains that can be added when cooking white or brown rice, an easy way to boost nutrition and fiber.

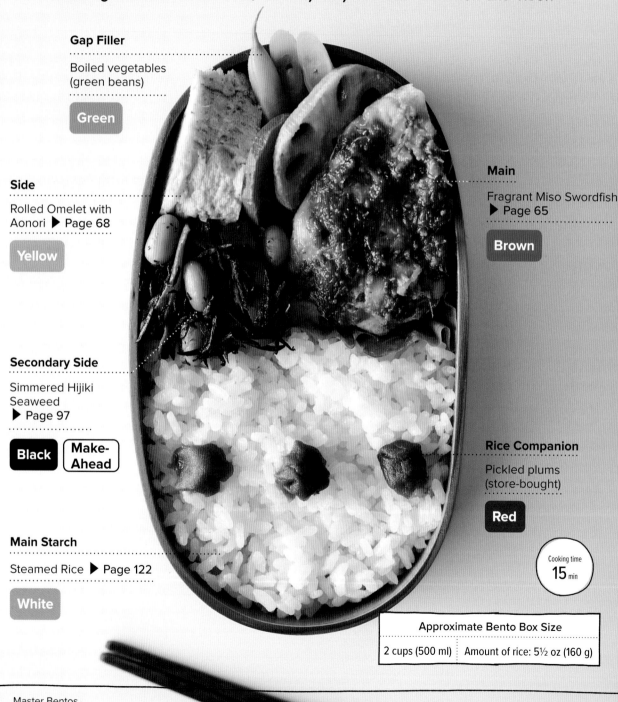

Gap Filler

Boiled vegetables
(green beans)

Green

Side

Rolled Omelet with
Aonori ▶ Page 68

Yellow

Secondary Side

Simmered Hijiki
Seaweed
▶ Page 97

Black | Make-Ahead

Main Starch

Steamed Rice ▶ Page 122

White

Main

Fragrant Miso Swordfish
▶ Page 65

Brown

Rice Companion

Pickled plums
(store-bought)

Red

Cooking time
15 min

Approximate Bento Box Size	
2 cups (500 ml)	Amount of rice: 5½ oz (160 g)

Healthy Bento Rules

Use less rice, more veggies and protein

People watching their weight need to eat enough protein and fiber while watching their total calories. Do this by packing less rice but plenty of high-protein mains and egg-based sides, along with vegetable and seaweed secondary sides.

Choose low-fat, high-protein meats and seafood

Dieters sometimes avoid meat because it can be high in fat, but cuts that are low in fat and high in protein are a great addition to a low-calorie diet. I also recommend fish such as swordfish that contain DHA, which helps to burn fat.

For kids in middle and high school, provide at least 500 calories

Growing children and teens need an adequate amount of energy. Extreme diets can cause malnutrition and negatively affect growth. Be sure to provide bentos with at least 500 calories, including a good balance of carbs, protein, and sides.

TIP: Use healthy fats like flaxseed oil

If you cut out all fats when you're on a diet, your skin will suffer and your hair will lose its luster. It's important to consume oils rich in omega-3 rich fatty acid, such as flaxseed oil and perilla oil, available at some Asian groceries.

Timing Guide

Cook the swordfish and vegetables together in the toaster oven to save time!

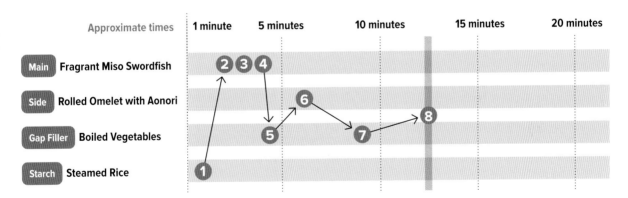

1. Pack warm rice into the bento box and leave it to cool.
2. Mix the miso sauce ingredients together.
3. Cut up the vegetables to cook with the main.
4. Start grilling the swordfish and vegetables.
5. Bring a small pot of salted water to a boil.
6. Make the Rolled Omelet with Aonori and leave to cool.
7. When the water has come to a boil, cook the green beans.
8. While the food cools, clean up. Pack the bento when everything is cool.

4

\ Try these tricks
to make it cute! /

Bentos For Young Children

Packing a bento to please a preschooler or early elementary student isn't just about how it looks. Nutrition, flavor, and the amount of food they can eat are all important, too.

Gap Filler

Baloney Flower ▶ Page 104

Red

Main

Japanese Style
Hamburgers ▶ Page 56

Brown

Secondary Side

Potato Salad ▶ Page 99

White

Side

Quail Eggs in Pepper
Rings ▶ Page 104

Green **Yellow**

Starch

Steamed Rice ▶ Page 122

White

Cooking time
20 min

Rice Companion

Furikake (store-bought)

Black

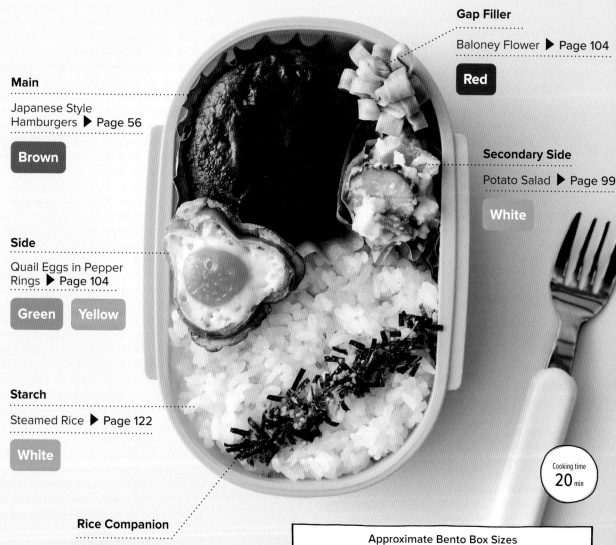

Approximate Bento Box Sizes		
For 4-year-olds:	1 cup (250 ml)	Amount of rice: 2⅔ oz (80 g)
For 5-year-olds:	1¼ cups (300 ml)	Amount of rice: 3½ oz (100 g)
For 6-year-olds:	1⅔ cups (400 ml)	Amount of rice: 4 oz (120 g)

Young Child Bento Rules

Pack an amount of food they can finish, and food they can eat easily

Kids get a sense of accomplishment from finishing their lunch, so pack just enough food for them. Make the food easier for them to eat by cutting it into small pieces or skewering it on picks.

For younger children, pack food they can eat with their hands

Put in utensils such as forks and spoons that match their level of development. For younger children, I recommend food that can be eaten with their hands such as small sandwiches.

Pack colorful, cute food

Colorful, cute foods like Quail Eggs in Pepper Rings and Baloney Flowers make eating lunch fun. Using food cutters to cut fruits and vegetables into shapes is another way to up the cuteness factor. You can buy sets of food cutters in many fun shapes online, or use mini cookie cutters.

Timing Guide

Double up on tasks like cutting and cooking.

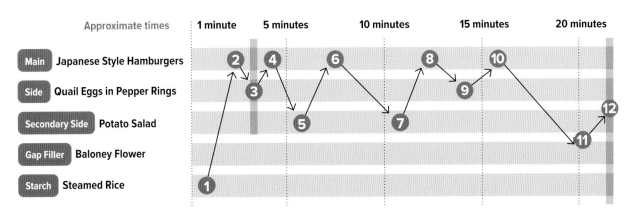

1. Pack warm rice into the bento box and leave it to cool.

2. Combine the seasonings for the hamburger.

3. Cut up the onions, bell pepper, carrot, cucumber and ham for the main and sides. Rub the cucumber with salt and squeeze out excess moisture.

4. Microwave the onions with butter for the main.

5. Cook the carrot and potato for the potato salad in the microwave.

6. Combine all the hamburger ingredients except the onion in a bowl.

7. Smash the potatoes and finish the potato salad.

8. When the onion has cooled, add to the hamburger mixture and form the burger.

9. Cook the Quail Eggs in Pepper Rings in a skillet. Remove from the skillet when done.

10. In the same skillet, cook the hamburger.

11. Cut the baloney flower.

12. While the food cools, clean up. Pack the bento when everything is cool.

5

\ A bento for the kid
who's always hungry! /

Bentos For Teenage Boys

When making bentos for this age group, remember that your child is
experiencing growth spurts and may have extracurricular activities.
Sports, in particular, require a lot of energy, so make sure
to tailor the menu to your child's activity level.

For boys who
don't play
sports

Side

Miso-Mayo Eggs
▶ Page 69

Brown **White**

Secondary Side

Okra with Smoky Fish
Flakes ▶ Page 89

Green

Secondary Side

Curried Squash
Crescents ▶ Page 82

Yellow

Starch

Steamed Rice ▶ Page 122

White

Gap Filler

Boiled vegetable
(broccoli)

Green

Main

Glazed Pork Steak
▶ Page 48

Brown

Rice Companion

Black sesame seeds

Black

Cooking time
25 min

	Approximate Bento Box Size
3 to 3⅓ cups (700 to 800 ml; 700 to 800 cal per meal)	Don't simply divide the amount of calories needed per day by three. Reduce calories for lunch slightly to account for snacks etc.
Amount of rice: 7 oz (200 g)	300 to 350 cal
Ratio of rice to other dishes: 1:1	2 Starch: 1 Main: 1 Side or 3 Starch: 1 Main: 2 Side

Teenage Boy Bento Rules

Don't give too many calories to kids who don't play sports

This is the time in their lives when kids need the most calories, about 2350 to 2750 per day. However, too many calories can cause obesity in boys who don't play sports.

For athletic boys, include foods that increase endurance and strength

Make sure the bento has plenty of carbs for energy to increase endurance and protein to build muscle. Also include green and yellow vegetables to relieve fatigue and prevent injuries.

Timing Guide ▶ Page 36

For boys who play sports

Use the same components, but up the serving size for carbs

Cooking time
25 min

Approximate Bento Box Size	
3⅓–4½ cups (800 to 1000 ml; 800 to 1000 cal per meal)	Don't simply divide the amount of calories needed per day by three. Reduce calories for lunch slightly to account for snacks etc.
Amount of Rice: 10½–12⅓ oz (300–350 g)	470 to 515 cal
Ratio of Rice to Other Dishes: 2.5 to 3: 2	2.5 Starch: 1 Main: 1 Side or 3 Starch: 1 Main: 2 Side

Full marks for color and nutritional balance!

Bentos For Teenage Girls

Although girls in middle and high school need fewer calories than boys, they still need enough energy and nutrients to support their growth. Don't forget to make their bentos look appetizing, too, by focusing on color and arrangement.

Main

Corn Kernel Meatballs
▶ Page 59

`Brown` `Yellow`

Bento for girls who don't play sports

Side

Imitation Crab Rolled Omelet
▶ Page 68

`Yellow` `Red` `White`

Secondary Side

Glazed Sweet Potato Chunks
▶ Page 85

`Yellow` `Make-Ahead`

Secondary Side

Stir-Fried Peppers with Tiny Fish ▶ Page 87

`Green`

Cooking time 15 min

Starch

Steamed Rice ▶ Page 122

`White`

Rice Companion

Bonito flakes and takuan pickles (store-bought)

`Brown` `Yellow`

Approximate Bento Box Size	
2 to 2⅓ cups (500 to 600 ml; 500 to 600 cal per meal)	Don't simply divide the amount of calories needed per day by three. Reduce calories for lunch slightly to account for snacks etc.
Amount of Rice: 5⅔–6⅓ oz (160 to 180 g)	300 to 350 cal
Ratio of rice to other dishes: 1:1	2 Starch: 1 Main: 1 Side or 3 Starch: 1 Main: 2 Side

Teenage Girl Bento Rules

Make sure girls who don't play sports get enough nutrition
Adolescents who are concerned about their bodies sometimes go on extreme diets. This is especially true for those who don't play sports, so be sure to support their growth with nutritionally balanced bentos.

Bentos for athletic girls should have a good, colorful balance between carbs and protein
Girls who play sports burn a lot of calories and need to eat the right amount of carbs and protein. They should have a balanced bento that is high in these nutrients. Make sure it has a good color balance, too.

Timing Guide ▶ Page 36

Use the same components, but increase the amounts

Bento for girls who play sports

Cooking time
15 min

Approximate Bento Box Size	
2 to 3⅓ cups (600 to 800 ml; 600 to 800 cal per meal)	Don't simply divide the amount of calories needed per day by three. Reduce calories for lunch slightly to account for snacks etc.
Amount of Rice: 8 oz (200 to 230 g)	310 to 360 cal
Ratio of Rice to Other Dishes: 2.5–3:2	2.5 Starch: 1 Main: 1 Side or 3 Starch: 1 Main: 1 Side

Timing Guide for Teenage Boy Bento

Use a skillet and a toaster oven to cook food at the same time.

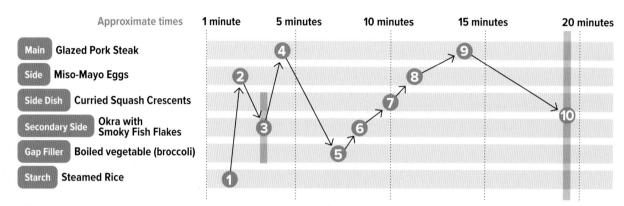

| | | Approximate times | 1 minute | 5 minutes | 10 minutes | 15 minutes | 20 minutes |

Main Glazed Pork Steak
Side Miso-Mayo Eggs
Side Dish Curried Squash Crescents
Secondary Side Okra with Smoky Fish Flakes
Gap Filler Boiled vegetable (broccoli)
Starch Steamed Rice

1. Pack warm rice into bento box to cool.
2. Boil the egg. Bring another small pot of water to boil on another burner.
3. Cut up the kabocha and broccoli. Roll the okra hard on a cutting board sprinkled with a little salt to remove the surface hairs.
4. Combine the seasonings for the Glazed Pork Steak.
5. Boil the broccoli and okra in the small pot.
6. Make the Okra with Smoky Fish Flakes.
7. Cook the Curried Squash Crescents in the skillet.
8. Bake the Miso-Mayo Eggs in the toaster oven.
9. Remove the squash from the skillet, wipe it out and cook the Glazed Pork Steak.
10. While the food cools, clean up. Pack the bento when everything is cool.

Timing Guide for Teenage Girl Bento

Cook one item in the microwave while you make another on the stove.

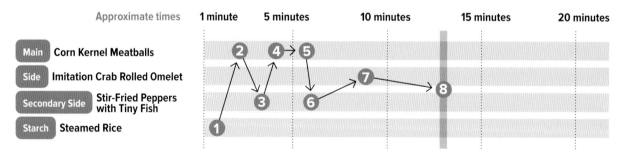

| | | Approximate times | 1 minute | 5 minutes | 10 minutes | 15 minutes | 20 minutes |

Main Corn Kernel Meatballs
Side Imitation Crab Rolled Omelet
Secondary Side Stir-Fried Peppers with Tiny Fish
Starch Steamed Rice

1. Pack warm rice into bento box to cool.
2. Cut up the onion for the Corn Kernel Meatballs.
3. Cut up the bell pepper for the Stir-Fried Peppers with Tiny Fish.
4. Combine the ingredients for Corn Kernel Meatballs and form into balls.
5. Cook the meatballs in the microwave.
6. Cook the peppers and tiny fish in a skillet.
7. Cook the Imitation Crab Rolled Omelet in another pan.
8. While the food cools, clean up. Pack the bento when everything is cool.

Part 1
Main Dishes

Chicken • Pork • Beef • Ground Meat • Seafood

The main dishes in this chapter, organized by ingredient,
go well with rice and taste great even when cold.
You'll find tips and photos to make cooking these tasty
dishes a snap. Don't forget to try the variations, too.

My Approach to Mains

The main dish in a bento should taste good when cold or at room temperature and should provide healthy protein. On the facing page, you'll find tips for success with simple, satisfying mains.

1. Aim to use just one pot or skillet when cooking the main

Save time in the morning by using a minimum of cooking equipment to cut down on clean-up. For mains, cooking in a skillet is especially convenient. This chapter includes recipes that can be cooked entirely in a microwave or toaster oven, too.

2. Use starch or flour to thicken liquids

You might assume that stir-fried, pan-fried and baked foods don't have much liquid, but seasonings like soy sauce and the liquid from vegetables can make them surprisingly moist. Dusting meat or fish with cornstarch or other thickeners before adding the seasonings helps flavors adhere to the food and reduces moisture, preventing spoilage at room temperature.

3. Cooking food thoroughly is key

When cooking meat, seafood or eggs for a bento, the key is to cook them thoroughly. Most bacteria, viruses and parasites cannot withstand heat and die when cooked. Pre-cooked foods such as ham and fishcakes should also be heated through in the summer.

4. Deep-fry in a small amount of oil

When making deep-fried foods such as karaage fried chicken or fried shrimp, use just enough oil to cover about half the ingredients; it makes dealing with the frying oil afterwards much easier. If you strain the oil right after using it and store it in a cool, dark place, you can reuse it two to three times.

5. Focus on flavors that go well with rice and taste good when cold

Flavors can become muted when cold, so I recommend seasoning heavily to accent plain steamed rice. You can use store-bought Japanese sauces like yakiniku sauce or mentsuyu (see Glossary of Japanese Ingredients, page 140). In winter, avoid dishes with fats that congeal when cold, such as animal fats and butter.

6. When cooking for small children, cut foods into easy-to-eat pieces

When preparing the recipes in this book for small children, cut the food into pieces that will fit their mouths. Avoid meat and fish dishes with bones. Also, use picks and cups to make the food look cute.

7. If you have spare time, make extra and store it in individual portions

The recipes in this chapter are basically intended to be prepared on the same day the bento will be eaten, but recipes marked "Make-Ahead" can be doubled and the extra portions used another day. It is convenient to freeze and label individual portions that fit the gender, age, and appetite of the person who will be eating the bento.

TIP: Do Step 1 of the recipe and combine the sauce ingredients the night before. In the morning, all that's left is to dust the chicken with flour and pan-fry it, slashing the prep time.

Chicken Teriyaki

Chicken thickly coated in a delicious sweet-and-savory sauce is a perfect partner for rice. A few key steps before cooking enhance the juicy umami of the chicken.

Per serving
449
cal

Cooking time
15 min

Make-Ahead

Keeps in the fridge for
3 days

Keeps in the freezer for
1 month

1 boneless chicken thigh,
  about 5 oz (150 g)
Salt and pepper
Flour for coating
2 teaspoons vegetable oil

Sauce*
2 teaspoons soy sauce
2 teaspoons sugar
2 teaspoons sake

Mustard Chicken

Cut **4 oz (120 g) of chicken thigh meat** into bite-size pieces. Sprinkle with **salt and pepper** and **½ tablespoon of flour**, in that order. Heat **1 tablespoon vegetable oil** in a small skillet over medium heat and pan-fry the chicken for about 8 minutes. When the chicken is cooked through, add **one teaspoon each of soy sauce, honey, sake and whole grain mustard** and toss to coat the chicken.

*2 tablespoons of store-bought yakiniku sauce can be substituted for the Sauce ingredients in the main recipe.

This step is the key to removing gaminess and improving flavor!

Cut away any excess fat or sinew from the chicken.

Flour seals in umami and helps the sauce coat the chicken.

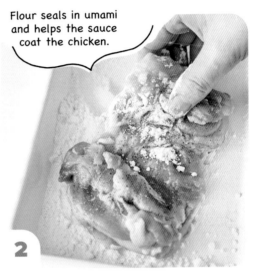

Sprinkle the trimmed chicken with salt, pepper and flour, in that order.

The skin becomes crispy and the meat becomes juicy.

Heat the oil in a small skillet over medium heat. Cook the chicken skin-side down for about 4 minutes. Flip and cook for 2 to 3 minutes more.

Combine the Sauce ingredients the day before for an easier morning!

Finished!

Combine the Sauce ingredients in a small bowl. When the chicken is cooked through, add the Sauce and reduce, turning the chicken to coat.

TIP: To test for the right oil temp without a thermometer, look for bubbles to form around an uncoated wooden chopstick dipped into the oil for one second. The chicken is done when the bubbles around it turn small and you hear a crackling sound.

Per serving	Cooking time		Keeps in the fridge for	Keeps in the freezer for
550 cal	10 min*	Make-Ahead	3 days	1 month*

Karaage Fried Chicken

This is a standard and widely loved bento item in Japan. The secret is the ginger and sesame oil used to pre-season the chicken.

SERVES 1

1 boneless chicken thigh, about 5 oz (150 g)
2 tablespoons cornstarch or potato starch
2 tablespoons pastry flour
Vegetable oil for frying

Marinade
½ tablespoon soy sauce
½ tablespoon sake
1 teaspoon grated ginger
1 teaspoon sesame oil
Salt and pepper

1 Cut the chicken into bite-sized pieces and toss with the Marinade ingredients. Place in a covered container and refrigerate for at least one hour and as long as overnight.

2 Combine the starch and flour, drain the marinated chicken, and dust with the starch and flour (see photo).
3 Put about 1 inch (2.5 cm) oil in a saucepan and heat to 355°F (180°C; see Tip). Fry the chicken until dark golden brown, 4 to 5 minutes.

Combining flour and starch makes for a crispy, light breading.

VARIATION:

Korean Style Fried Chicken

Cut **4 oz (120 g) boneless chicken breast** into strips and toss with **a dash of pepper, 2 teaspoons sake, and a grated garlic clove**. Dust the chicken with **cornstarch** and fry in 355 °F (180 °C; see Tip) oil. Combine **½ tablespoon gochujang** (Korean spicy bean paste), **½ tablespoon ketchup, 1 teaspoon sugar, 1 teaspoon sake and 1 teaspoon mirin** in a small skillet and bring to a simmer. Add the fried chicken and stir to coat. Sprinkle with **toasted white sesame seeds**.

*Cooking time does not include marinating the chicken. The raw, seasoned chicken can be frozen with or without the coating. It should be fried the day it will be eaten.

Per serving **140** cal · Cooking time **18** min · Make-Ahead · Keeps in the fridge for **3** days · Keeps in the freezer for **1** month

Chicken Roll

Steam after browning for a moist finish.

SERVES 2 TO 4

10 oz (300 g) boneless chicken breast
Salt
2 teaspoons vegetable oil
1 clove garlic
1 knob ginger

Sauce
1 tablespoon soy sauce
1 tablespoon sake
1 tablespoon mirin
½ cup (100 ml) water

1 Butterfly the chicken breast and pound to an even thickness. Sprinkle lightly with salt, roll up from the side nearest you, and tie with kitchen twine (see photo). Thinly slice the garlic and ginger.

2 Heat the vegetable oil over moderately high heat in a medium skillet and brown the Chicken Roll on all sides.
3 Add the Sauce ingredients, garlic, and ginger to the pan. Cover and steam over low heat for about 10 minutes.
4 Remove lid, cook off excess moisture, and coat the meat with sauce.

VARIATION:

Lemon Chicken Roll

For the Sauce, substitute **1 tablespoon lemon juice, 3 tablespoons white wine, ½ tablespoon granulated bouillon** and **½ cup (100 ml) water**. Omit ginger and use **2 cloves garlic,** sliced. Cook as for the Chicken Roll.

Wrap the kitchen twine tightly from one end to prevent the Chicken Roll from falling apart.

Chicken with Mushrooms and Tomato Sauce

Packed with umami, this stew is tasty even when cold. White or cremini mushrooms can be substituted for shimeji and maitake.

SERVES 2 TO 4

2 boneless chicken thighs,
  about 10 oz (300 g)
Salt and pepper
Flour for coating
½ onion
4 oz (100 g) shimeji mushrooms
4 oz (100 g) maitake mushrooms
1 tablespoon olive oil
1 garlic clove
1 dried red chili pepper, seeded
14 oz (400 g) can chopped
  tomatoes
2 tablespoons sake or white wine
1 tablespoon sugar
2 teaspoons granulated bouillon
1 cup (200 ml) water

1 Cut the chicken into bite-size pieces. Sprinkle with salt, pepper and flour in that order. Slice the onion thinly. Cut the stem ends off the mushrooms and divide into small clumps.

2 Warm the oil, garlic and chili in a medium skillet over low heat. When the oil smells fragrant remove the garlic and chili and add the chicken, skin side down. Cook for about 2 minutes on each side. Stir-fry the onion on one side of the skillet at the same time.

3 When both sides of the chicken are browned, add the mushrooms and stir-fry briefly, incorporating the onions. Add the canned tomato, sake or wine, sugar, granulated bouillon and water. Simmer until there is almost no liquid left in the skillet. Season to taste with salt and pepper.

Per serving
235 cal

Cooking time
12 min

Make-Ahead

Keeps in the fridge for
3 days

Keeps in the freezer for
1 month

Breaded Chicken and Bell Pepper

Bell pepper adds color and nutrition to this simple dish.

SERVES 1

½ skinless chicken breast,
  about 4 oz (100 g)
Scant ¼ teaspoon salt
Black pepper
1 teaspoon sake
⅓ red bell pepper
1 egg
Vegetable oil for cooking
1½ tablespoons flour

1 Thinly slice the chicken and rub with the salt, pepper and sake. Cut the bell pepper into strips about 1 inch (2.5 cm) wide. Beat the egg in a shallow bowl.

2 Heat about ¼ inch (6 mm) of oil in a medium skillet over medium heat. Dust the chicken and peppers with flour and dip each piece in the beaten egg. Fry until the egg coating is dry. Remove from the skillet, dip in egg again, and fry again. Repeat two to three times.

3 Fry the bell pepper until lightly browned, remove from the skillet and salt lightly. Fry the chicken until cooked through, about 2 minutes.

Per serving
378 cal

Cooking time
10 min

Make-Ahead

Keeps in the fridge
2 days

Keeps in the freezer
1 month

Chicken with Oyster Sauce

This healthy mix of vegetables and chicken is richly flavored and satisfying.

SERVES 1

2 chicken tenders, about 4 oz (100 g)
Salt and pepper
Flour for coating
1 king oyster mushroom
5 green beans
1 tablespoon vegetable oil

Sauce
½ tablespoon oyster sauce
½ teaspoon soy sauce
1 teaspoon mirin
1 teaspoon sake

1 Remove the tendons from the chicken tenders and cut into 1½-inch (3 to 4 cm) strips. Sprinkle with salt, pepper and flour in that order. Quarter the mushroom lengthwise and halve crosswise. Slice the green beans diagonally into 3 or 4 pieces.

2 Heat the vegetable oil in a skillet over medium heat and stir-fry the chicken for about 2 minutes. Add the green beans and mushroom and stir-fry with the chicken for another 2 to 3 minutes.
3 When the chicken is cooked through, add the combined Sauce ingredients and cook briefly to coat.

Per serving
285 cal

Cooking time
10 min

Make-Ahead

Keeps in the fridge for
3 days

Keeps in the freezer for
1 month

Tandoori Chicken

Marinating the chicken the day before doesn't just save time in the morning—it makes the chicken incredibly tasty and tender.

SERVES 3

6 chicken drumsticks, about 12 oz (350 g)

Marinade
4 tablespoons plain yogurt
1 tablespoon ketchup
½ tablespoon curry powder
1 teaspoon grated garlic
1 teaspoon grated ginger
½ teaspoon salt
Black pepper

1 Combine the Marinade ingredients in a bowl, add the chicken and marinate for at least an hour, preferably overnight.
2 Broil the chicken for 10 to 12 minutes, covering with aluminum foil partway

through if the chicken begins to brown.
To cook in a toaster oven, place the drumsticks on a baking sheet and bake for 12 to 15 minutes until browned and cooked through.

Per drumstick
117 cal

Cooking time *
20 min

Make-Ahead

Keeps in the fridge for
3 days

Keeps in the freezer for
1 month

*Does not include marinating time.

Ginger Pork

Coated with a thick, gingery sauce, the pork stays juicy when cold. Ginger stimulates the appetite and may also have antimicrobial qualities. The variation uses shirataki noodles, available in the refrigerator section of Asian groceries.

Per serving
452
cal

Cooking time
10 min

Make-Ahead

Keeps in the fridge for
3 days

Keeps in the freezer for
1 month

3 thin slices of fatty pork loin,
    about 4 oz (120 g)
Salt and pepper
⅛ onion
1 teaspoon flour
2 teaspoons vegetable oil

Sauce
1 teaspoon grated ginger
1 tablespoon sake
1 tablespoon mirin

VARIATION

Simmered Pork with Shirataki Noodles

Cut **4 oz (120 g) of very thinly sliced pork belly** into bite-size pieces. Slice **2 green beans** diagonally and cut **2 oz (50 g) of shirataki noodles** into 1-inch (3-cm) pieces. Heat a skillet over medium heat and stir-fry the pork and green beans, adding the shirataki noodles once the meat has changed color. Add **2 teaspoons soy sauce, 2 teaspoons mirin, 1 teaspoon sugar** and **½ teaspoon grated ginger.** Simmer to reduce the liquid.

TIP: Thickening the sauce with flour not only improves flavor and texture, it also helps prevent messy spills when transporting your bento.

Cut each slice of pork into bite-size pieces.

1

Cut each slice of pork into 3 equal pieces and sprinkle with salt and pepper. Thinly slice the onion.

Spread out the pork slices when you put them in the pan. Chopsticks work well for this!

2

Heat the vegetable oil in a skillet and stir-fry the pork and onion for 2 to 3 minutes.

Adding flour helps the sauce coat the pork.

3

When the onion is wilted and the meat has changed color, sprinkle in the flour.

Measure and mix the seasonings in advance to save time.

Finished!

4

When the flour is well distributed, add the combined Sauce ingredients and cook briefly to coat.

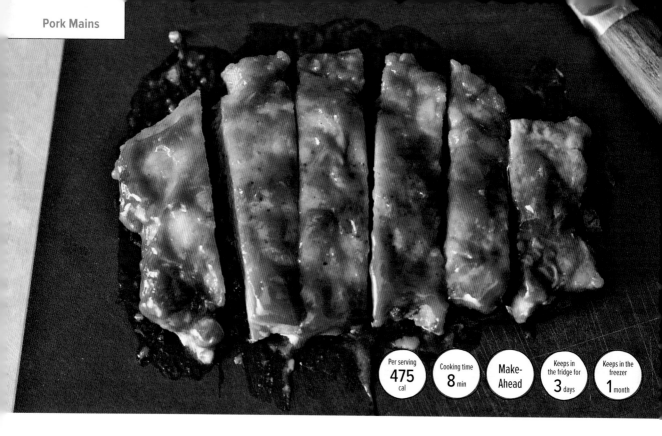

Per serving
475 cal

Cooking time
8 min

Make-Ahead

Keeps in the fridge for
3 days

Keeps in the freezer
1 month

Glazed Pork Steak

Tender meat and a sweet sauce make this pork a hit with kids. Worcestershire sauce can be substituted for the tonkatsu sauce.

SERVES 1

1 thin boneless pork loin chop, about 4 oz (120 g)
Flour for dusting
2 teaspoons vegetable oil

Sauce
1 tablespoon ketchup
1 tablespoon tonkatsu sauce
1 tablespoon sake
½ tablespoon French mustard
1 teaspoon honey

1 Pound the meat with the spine of a kitchen knife (see photo), then sprinkle with flour.
2 Heat the vegetable oil in a small skillet and fry the pork for about 2 minutes on each side.
3 When the pork is cooked through, add the combined Sauce ingredients and turn to coat.

Breaking the fibers of the meat tenderizes it.

| Per serving **504** cal | Cooking time **15** min | **Make-Ahead** | Keeps in the fridge for **2** days | Keeps in the freezer for **1** month |

Pork & Vegetable Rolls

The orange and green of this simply seasoned dish brighten up any bento box. Bacon can be substituted for the pork belly, but omit the salt.

Keep the cross-section in mind when arranging the veggies in the roll.

SERVES 1

4 thin slices pork belly,
    about 12 inch (30 cm) long;
    4 oz (120 g) total
⅓ teaspoon salt
Pepper
Flour for dusting
4 pieces carrot, cut into
    5 x ⅓ inch (12 x 1 cm) sticks
4 green beans
1 teaspoon vegetable oil

1 Place the carrot sticks in a small pan of cold water, bring to a boil and cook for 4 to 5 minutes. Add the green beans for the last 2 minutes. Drain.
2 Cut the pork belly slices in half lengthwise and line up 4 slices on a cutting board.

Sprinkle with salt and pepper. Lay half the boiled vegetables across the near end and roll up (see photo). Dust with flour. Repeat for the second roll.
3 Heat the vegetable oil in a small skillet over medium heat and place the rolls in the pan seam side down. Brown all sides.
4 Cover and steam for 3 to 4 minutes. Remove and slice into bite-size pieces.

VARIATION:

Pork-Wrapped Winter Squash

Slice **3 oz (80 g) seeded kabocha or other winter squash** into ⅓ inch (8 mm) thick slices. Wrap the slices with **4 oz (100 g) thinly sliced pork belly**. Dust with **flour**. Heat **1 teaspoon vegetable oil** in a small skillet over medium heat and place the rolls in the pan seam-side down. Fry 5 to 6 minutes, turning midway. Add **½ tablespoon soy sauce, ½ tablespoon mirin, ½ tablespoon sake** and **half a clove of garlic**, grated. Coat the rolls with the sauce.

Stir-Fried Pork with Vegetables

Cut up the vegetables and mix the sauce
the day before to save time.

SERVES 1

2 cabbage leaves
1 small green bell pepper
3 thin slices pork loin, about 3 oz
    (90 g)
Salt and pepper
½ tablespoon cornstarch or potato
    starch
1 teaspoon sesame oil
Coarsely ground black pepper

Sauce
¼ teaspoon doubanjiang (spicy
    Chinese bean paste)
½ teaspoon soy sauce
2 teaspoons sake
2 teaspoons mirin
1 teaspoon miso

1 Cut the cabbage into 1½ inch (3 to 4 cm) squares. Seed the bell pepper and cut into big pieces. Cut the pork into 1½ inch (3 to 4 cm) wide pieces and sprinkle with salt, pepper and starch in that order.
2 Heat the sesame oil in a medium skillet and stir-fry the pork for 1 to 2 minutes. When the meat changes color, add the vegetables and toss to coat with oil.
3 Combine the Sauce ingredients, add to the pan and continue to stir-fry briefly. Season with the black pepper.

Per serving
391 cal

Cooking time
10 min

Make-Ahead

Keeps in the fridge for
3 days

Keeps in the freezer for
1 month

Sweet and Sour Pork

Precooking the carrot in the microwave shortens stir-frying time.

SERVES 1

1 thin piece pork loin, about 4 oz
    (100 g)
Salt and pepper
1 teaspoon cornstarch or potato
    starch
1-inch (3-cm) piece carrot
1 small green bell pepper
¼ onion
2 teaspoons vegetable oil

Sauce
1 teaspoon rice vinegar
1 teaspoon soy sauce
1 teaspoon sugar
1 teaspoon mirin
1½ tablespoons ketchup
½ teaspoon cornstarch or potato
    starch

1 Cut the pork into bite-size pieces and sprinkle with salt, pepper and starch in that order. Cut the carrot into chunks. Seed the bell pepper and roughly chop. Cut the onion into ¾ inch (2 cm) squares.
2 Put the carrot pieces in a heatproof bowl, cover with cling film and microwave for 50 seconds.
3 Heat the vegetable oil in a medium skillet. Stir-fry the pork over medium heat on one side of the pan for about 2 minutes. Stir-fry the bell pepper and onion on the other half of the skillet. When the meat is cooked through, add the carrots and the combined Sauce ingredients and cook briefly to coat.

Per serving
458 cal

Cooking time
10 min

Make-Ahead

Keeps in the fridge for
3 days

Keeps in the freezer for
1 month

Pork Skewers

These cook nicely in a toaster oven, freeing up the stovetop for other dishes.

SERVES 1 (2 SKEWERS)

4 oz (100 g) pork belly
Salt
¼ teaspoon granulated chicken
   bouillon
Coarsely ground black pepper

1 Cut the pork into ⅓ inch (1 cm) thick pieces and sprinkle with the salt, chicken soup stock granules and coarsely ground black pepper.
2 Place the pork chunks on a baking sheet and bake in a toaster oven for 7 to 8 minutes until browned and cooked through.
3 Skewer the Step 2 pork on skewers for easy eating.

TIP: The pork will release a lot of fat when cooking, so it's a good idea to set a grill on top of the baking sheet to let the fat drain off. Red or pink juice is a sign the pork is undercooked and should be baked for 1 to 2 minutes longer.

Per skewer
200 cal

Cooking time
15 min

Make-Ahead

Keeps in the fridge for
3 days

Keeps in the freezer for
1 month

Mini Pork Cutlets

Bite-size for easy eating.

SERVES 1

4 oz (100 g) thinly sliced pork
¼ teaspoon salt
Black pepper
1 teaspoon cornstarch or potato starch
Flour for coating
1 egg, beaten
4 tablespoons panko breadcrumbs
Vegetable oil for frying

1 Cut the pork into small pieces. Sprinkle with salt, pepper and starch in that order. Form into four equal patties.
2 Coat the patties with flour, beaten egg and breadcrumbs in that order.
3 Heat 1 inch (2.5 cm) of oil in a small skillet to 355 °F (180 °C; see Tip page 42). Fry the patties until golden brown, 4 to 5 minutes.

*The breaded meat can be frozen before frying. When ready to use, fry without defrosting.

Per cutlet
91 cal

Cooking time
10 min

Make-Ahead

Keeps in the fridge for
3 days

Keeps in the freezer for *
1 month

Per serving
355 cal

Cooking time
8 min

Make-Ahead

Keeps in the fridge for
3 days

Keeps in the freezer for
1 month

Stir-Fried Beef with Peppers

Red and green bell peppers and bamboo shoots make this dish pop.

SERVES 1

3 oz (80 g) thinly sliced beef round
1 teaspoon soy sauce
1 teaspoon sake
½ tablespoon cornstarch or potato starch
1 small red bell pepper
1 small green bell pepper
1½ oz (40 g) canned bamboo shoot strips
2 teaspoons vegetable oil
2 teaspoons mirin
2 teaspoons oyster sauce

1 Cut the beef into thin strips and toss with the soy sauce, sake and starch (see photo). Seed the bell peppers and thinly slice.

2 Heat the vegetable oil in a skillet over medium heat, add the beef and stir-fry for about 2 minutes. When the meat changes color, add the bell pepper and bamboo shoot.

3 When the vegetables are coated with oil, add the mirin and oyster sauce and cook briefly.

Pre-seasoning the beef adds an extra layer of flavor.

Per serving
154 cal

Cooking time
8 min

Make-Ahead

Keeps in the fridge for
2 days

Keeps in the freezer for
1 month

Stir-Fried Beef with Ketchup

This dish has just the right balance of sweet and tart flavors. It's good with bread as well as rice.

SERVES 1 TO 2

4 oz (100 g) thinly sliced beef
4 to 5 broccoli florets
2 teaspoons vegetable oil
1 teaspoon flour
2 tablespoons ketchup
1 teaspoon Worcestershire
  sauce

1 Halve or quarter the broccoli florets and place in a small pan with 3 to 4 tablespoons water. Cover and steam over medium heat for 2 minutes. Remove from pan and wipe the pan dry.
2 Add the vegetable oil and stir-fry the beef over medium heat for 1 to 2 minutes. When the beef is cooked through, sprinkle with flour (see photo).
3 When the flour is well distributed, add the broccoli, ketchup and Worcestershire sauce and stir-fry briefly to combine.

Thickening with flour helps the flavor adhere to the meat and veggies.

VARIATION:

Curried Beef and Bell Pepper

Cut **1 small bell pepper** into ½ inch (1.5 cm) wide pieces. Thinly slice **¼ onion**. Heat **1 teaspoon vegetable oil** over medium heat in a skillet and stir-fry the bell pepper, onion and **4 oz (100 g) thinly sliced beef**. When the onion has softened, add **1 teaspoon curry powder**, **½ tablespoon soy sauce**, **½ tablespoon sake** and **½ tablespoon mirin** and stir-fry briefly to combine.

Beef and Cheese Rolls

The combination of juicy beef and melted cheese is super satisfying.

SERVES 1 (4 ROLLS)

4 oz (120 g) thinly sliced beef short rib
Salt and pepper
1½ oz (40 g) processed cheese
Flour for coating
1 egg, beaten
4 tablespoons panko breadcrumbs
Vegetable oil for frying

1 Divide the beef into 4 portions, spread flat, and sprinkle with salt and pepper. Place a quarter of the cheese on each piece of beef and wrap so the cheese is hidden.
2 Coat the beef bundles with flour, beaten egg and breadcrumbs in that order.
3 Heat about 1 inch (2.5 cm) of oil in a skillet to 355 °F (180 °C; see Tip page 42). Fry the bundles until golden, 3 to 4 minutes.

*Rolls may be frozen before frying. When ready to use, fry without defrosting.

Per roll
181 cal

Cooking time
10 min

Make-Ahead

Keeps in the fridge for
2 days

Keeps in the freezer for *
1 month

Soy Simmered Beef

For tender results, make sure to add the sugar at the right time.

SERVES 1

2-inch (5-cm) piece burdock root
4-inch (10-cm) piece fat green onion
3 oz (80 g) thinly sliced beef
2 teaspoons vegetable oil
1 teaspoon sugar

Sauce
1 tablespoon sake
2 teaspoons soy sauce
2 teaspoons mirin
3 tablespoons water

1 Sliver the burdock root and slice the green onion diagonally. Cut the beef into bite-size pieces.
2 Heat the vegetable oil in a skillet, stir-fry the beef for about 2 minutes, and add the sugar.
3 When the beef is cooked through, add the burdock root and green onion and stir-fry briefly. Add the combined Sauce ingredients and simmer until the liquid is gone.

Per serving
283 cal

Cooking time
10 min

Make-Ahead

Keeps in the fridge for
3 to **4** days

Keeps in the freezer for
1 month

Glass Noodles with Beef

Cooking in the microwave makes this tasty Korean dish a snap.

SERVES 1

⅛ onion
1 small green bell pepper
1-inch (3-cm) piece carrot
2 oz (50 g) thinly sliced beef
½ oz (15 g) glass noodles
Toasted white sesame seeds

Sauce
½ teaspoon doubanjiang (Chinese spicy bean paste)
2 tablespoons yakiniku sauce
⅓ cup (80 ml) water

1 Thinly slice the onion. Seed the bell pepper and slice thinly. Cut the carrot into thin rectangles. If the beef slices are large, cut them into bite-size pieces.
2 Combine the beef, glass noodles, vegetables and Sauce ingredients in a heatproof bowl. Cover with cling film and microwave for 3 minutes. Mix well and microwave for another 2 minutes. Let rest, still covered.
3 When all the moisture has been absorbed, sprinkle with sesame seeds.

*Cooking time does not include resting time.

Per serving
225 cal

Cooking time*
10 min

Make-Ahead

Keeps in the fridge for
3 days

Keeps in the freezer for
1 month

Citrusy Beef and Asparagus

The refreshing tartness of ponzu sauce pairs perfectly with the sweetness of honey.

SERVES 1

2 asparagus stalks
3 oz (80 g) thinly sliced boneless beef short rib
Salt and pepper
1 teaspoon sesame oil
1 tablespoon ponzu sauce
1 teaspoon honey

1 Remove the tough ends of the asparagus and slice diagonally. Sprinkle the beef with salt and pepper.
2 Heat the sesame oil in a skillet over medium heat and cook the beef for about 1 minute per side. Meanwhile, stir-fry the asparagus in a corner of the pan.

3 When the beef is browned on both sides and the asparagus is cooked through, add the ponzu sauce and honey and stir-fry briefly to combine all ingredients.

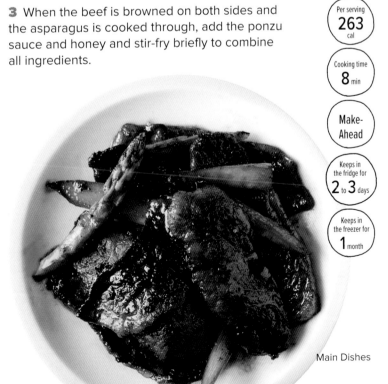

Per serving
263 cal

Cooking time
8 min

Make-Ahead

Keeps in the fridge for
2 to **3** days

Keeps in the freezer for
1 month

Per burger	Cooking time		Keeps in the fridge for	Keeps in the freezer for
230 cal	**20** min	Make-Ahead	**3** to **4** days	**1** month

Japanese Style Hamburgers

If you are making these for small children, divide the meat into three or four burgers before cooking, instead of two.

SERVES 1 (2 SMALL BURGERS)

¼ onion, finely minced
1 teaspoon butter
4 oz (100 g) ground beef-pork blend
½ beaten egg
2 tablespoons breadcrumbs
Salt and pepper
2 teaspoons vegetable oil

Sauce

1 tablespoon sake or red wine
1½ tablespoons ketchup
½ tablespoon tonkatsu sauce or Worcestershire sauce

1 Place the minced onion in a heatproof bowl with the butter (see photo), cover with cling film and microwave for 1 minute. Transfer to a plate or other shallow container to cool in the refrigerator for a few minutes.

2 In a bowl, thoroughly mix the ground meat, cooked onion, egg, breadcrumbs, salt and pepper. Form into 2 oval patties.

3 Heat the oil in a small skillet over medium heat. Fry patties for 2 minutes per side. When browned, cover and cook over low heat for about 3 minutes. Add the combined Sauce ingredients and reduce, coating the burgers.

Microwaving is an easy way to cook the onions. Cool well before adding to the meat.

VARIATION:

Cheesy Stuffed Shiitake Caps

Remove stems from **4 fresh shiitakes**, chop stems, and add to the meat along with the ingredients listed in main recipe. Dust insides of mushrooms caps with **cornstarch or potato starch** and stuff with the meat. Heat **2 teaspoons vegetable oil** in a skillet and cook the stuffed caps, meat side down, over medium heat until browned. Flip and cook over low heat for 3 minutes. Sprinkle with ½ **teaspoon soy sauce** and top each mushroom with ¼ of **a slice of processed cheese**.

Per patty	Cooking time	Make-Ahead	Keeps in the fridge for	Keeps in the freezer for
52 cal	10 min		3 days	1 month

Chicken Patties with Edamame

Frozen edamame are convenient for this recipe. Defrost and shell the beans the day before to make your morning easier.

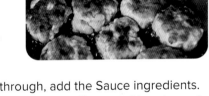

Thickening the sauce with starch helps the flavor coat the patties.

SERVES 2 (8 PATTIES)

4 oz (100 g) ground chicken
2-inch (5-cm) piece fat green onion, finely minced
2 tablespoons shelled edamame
2 teaspoons mayonnaise
Pinch of salt
½ tablespoon cornstarch or potato starch
1 tablespoon vegetable oil

Sauce
1 teaspoon soy sauce
1 teaspoon sake
1 teaspoon mirin
½ teaspoon sugar
1 tablespoon water

Thickener
½ teaspoon potato starch or cornstarch
1 tablespoon water

1 Place chicken, green onion, edamame, mayonnaise, salt, and starch in a bowl and mix well.
2 Heat the oil in a medium skillet and add spoonfuls of the chicken mixture. Cook for 2 minutes per side.
3 When browned and cooked through, add the Sauce ingredients. When bubbly add combined Thickener ingredients and turn to coat.

VARIATION:

Lotus Root with Ground Pork

Combine **4 oz (100 g) ground pork**, **½ teaspoon grated ginger, one green onion**, finely minced, **⅛ teaspoon salt, a pinch of black pepper** and **½ teaspoon cornstarch**. Cut a **3 inch (8 cm) piece of lotus root or potato** crosswise into thin slices, coat one side of each slice with cornstarch, and make sandwiches with the meat mixture (starched sides of lotus facing out). Heat 2 teaspoons vegetable oil in a skillet, add sandwiches, cover and cook over low for 5 minutes per side. Add **½ tablespoon soy sauce** and **1 tablespoon mirin** and cook briefly. Sprinkle with **toasted white sesame seeds**.

Stuffed Peppers

Thin-fleshed Japanese peppers work well here. Leaving the stems on prevents the juices from spilling out when you cook the peppers.

SERVES 1 TO 2 (4 PIECES)

2 Japanese green bell peppers or small bell peppers
Cornstarch or potato starch
4-inch (10-cm) piece fat green onion
4 oz (100 g) ground beef-pork blend
1 teaspoon mayonnaise
Salt and pepper
1 teaspoon breadcrumbs
2 tablespoons shredded pizza cheese

1 Halve the peppers lengthwise, seed, and sprinkle the insides lightly with starch. Finely mince the green onion.

2 Put the ground meat, minced green onion, mayonnaise, salt and pepper, and breadcrumbs in a bowl and mix well. Stuff the meat mixture into the bell peppers and top with cheese.

3 Place the bell peppers on a baking sheet and cook for 7 to 8 minutes in a toaster oven, until meat juices run clear.

Per piece **89** cal

Cooking time **15** min

Make-Ahead

Keeps in the fridge for **3** days

Keeps in the freezer for **1** month

Chicken Nuggets

These nuggets are dropped from a spoon into shallow oil, so they're very easy to make.

SERVES 2 (8 PIECES)

¼ onion
8 oz (240 g) ground chicken
1 teaspoon granulated bouillon
Salt and pepper
1 egg, beaten
2 tablespoons cornstarch or potato starch
Vegetable oil for frying

1 Grate the onion.

2 Put the ground chicken, grated onion, granulated bouillon, salt, pepper, beaten egg and starch in a bowl and mix well.

3 Heat about ¾ inch (2 cm) of oil in a skillet to 355 °F (180 °C; see Tip page 42). Drop spoonfuls of the chicken mixture into the oil and fry until golden brown.

Per nugget **87** cal

Cooking time **10** min

Make-Ahead

Keeps in the fridge for **3** to **4** days

Keeps in the freezer for **1** month

Corn Kernel Meatballs

Packed with corn kernels, these tasty meatballs are visually interesting, too.

SERVES 1 TO 2 (6 MEATBALLS)

⅛ **onion**
1 egg
4 oz (100 g) ground pork
Scant ¼ teaspoon salt
Black pepper
1 tablespoon breadcrumbs
Cornstarch or potato starch
Scant ½ cup (80 g) canned or frozen whole corn kernels

1 Mince the onion finely. Separate the egg and beat the whites lightly.
2 Put the ground pork, onion, egg yolk, salt, pepper and breadcrumbs in a bowl and mix well. Form into 6 equal balls. Dust lightly with starch, dip in the egg white, and sprinkle with the corn kernels.
3 Place the meatballs on a heatproof dish, cover with cling film and microwave for 2 minutes. Turn over and microwave for another minute.

Per meatball **64** cal

Cooking time **10** min

Make-Ahead

Keeps in the fridge for **3** days

Keeps in the freezer for **1** month

Tofu in Savory Meat Sauce

This recipe uses a thick fried tofu cutlet, available at Asian groceries, that doesn't need to be drained like regular tofu.

SERVES 1

1 atsuage tofu cutlet, about 5 oz (160 g)
1 small knob ginger
4 inch (10 cm) piece fat green onion
2 teaspoons vegetable oil
2 oz (60 g) ground pork
1 teaspoon cornstarch or potato starch

Sauce
½ **teaspoon doubanjiang (Chinese spicy bean paste)**
½ **teaspoon granulated chicken bouillon**
½ **tablespoon miso**
½ **tablespoon ketchup**
1 teaspoon sugar
½ **cup (100 ml) water**

1 Cut the tofu into ½ inch (1.5 cm) cubes. Finely mince the ginger and green onion.
2 Put the vegetable oil, ginger and half the green onion in a skillet and stir-fry over low heat for about a minute. When the oil is fragrant, increase the heat to medium, add the ground pork, and stir-fry. When the meat changes color, add the Sauce ingredients and the tofu and simmer for 1 to 2 minutes.
3 Sprinkle the remaining green onion with the starch and add to the skillet. Simmer until thickened.

Per serving **493** cal

Cooking time **10** min

Make-Ahead

Keeps in the fridge for **2** days

Fried Shrimp

Regular straight fried shrimp are hard to pack in a bento, but if you make them round like these they fit easily and look cute, too!

Per shrimp
53 cal

Cooking time
10 min

Make-Ahead

Keeps in the fridge for
2 days

Keeps in the freezer for
1 month

4 large shrimp
Salt and pepper
Flour for coating
1 egg, beaten
Panko breadcrumbs
Vegetable oil for frying

Cutting the shrimp open from the back makes deveining easier.

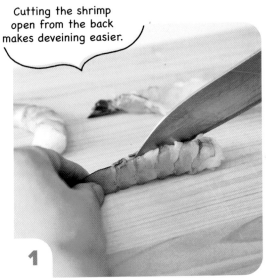

1

Peel the shrimp but leave the tails on. Butterfly by cutting along their backs.

Make sure to remove all of the vein, since it has a gritty texture and strong smell.

2

Use a toothpick to devein the shrimp. Sprinkle with salt and pepper.

Skewer the shrimp securely so they don't unfurl in the oil.

3

Roll up the shrimp starting from the head end and skewer with toothpicks. Coat with flour, beaten egg and breadcrumbs in that order.

Remove the shrimp from the oil as soon as they are golden brown.

Finished!

4

Heat 1 inch (2.5 cm) of oil in a skillet to 355 °F (180 °C; see Tip page 42). Fry the shrimp until golden brown, 2 to 3 minutes. Remove the toothpicks before packing in the bento box.

Per serving
350 cal

Cooking time
10 min *

Make-Ahead

Keeps in the fridge for
2 to **3** days

Keeps in the freezer for
1 month

Teriyaki Fish Steak

Great with steamed rice. Try salmon, tuna or swordfish in place of the yellowtail, also called amberjack.

SERVES 1

1 small yellowtail (*buri*) steak or other firm, mild fish, about 3 oz (80 g)
Salt
Cornstarch or potato starch
2 teaspoons vegetable oil

Sauce
½ tablespoon soy sauce
½ tablespoon sake
½ tablespoon mirin
1 teaspoon sugar

1 Sprinkle the yellowtail with salt and let rest 8 to 9 minutes. Blot excess moisture with paper towels (see photo) and sprinkle with starch.
2 Heat the vegetable oil in a skillet and cook the yellowtail over medium heat until lightly browned, about 2 to 3 minutes. Flip and fry for another minute.
3 When the fish is cooked through, add the combined Sauce ingredients and cook until the sauce is reduced and coats the fish.

*Does not include salting and resting time.

Removing excess moisture reduces fishy smells.

TIP: If you're short on time, skip the salting process and pour boiling water over the fish instead; this is another way to eliminate unpleasant fishy smells. Pat dry and sprinkle with starch.

Per serving **230** cal | Cooking time **10** min * | **Make-Ahead** | Keeps in the fridge for **3** days | Keeps in the freezer for **1** month

Gingery Fried Mackerel

Try bluefish, mahi mahi, or other types of mackerel if you can't find fresh or frozen Spanish mackerel.

SERVES 1

3 oz (80 g) Spanish mackerel (sawara) or other fatty, strongly flavored fish
Cornstarch or potato starch
Vegetable oil for frying

Marinade
½ tablespoon soy sauce
½ tablespoon sake
1 teaspoon ginger juice (made by squeezing grated ginger)

1 Cut the fish into bite-size pieces. Toss with Marinade ingredients and leave for about 10 minutes, then dust with starch (see photo).
2 Heat ¾ inch (2 cm) of oil in a skillet to 355 °F (180 °C; see Tip page 42). Fry the fish until golden brown, about 3 minutes.

Dust the fish with starch just before frying.

VARIATION:

Gingery Fried Salmon

Replace the Spanish mackerel with salmon and follow instructions in the main recipe.

*Does not include marinating time.

Breadcrumb Topped Salmon

Brown the flavorful breadcrumbs
so they look appetizing.

SERVES 1

4 oz (100 g) salmon
Salt and pepper

Topping
1 tablespoon panko breadcrumbs
1 teaspoon olive oil
¼ teaspoon dried parsley flakes
Salt
Garlic powder
Coarsely ground black pepper

1 Cut the salmon into 3 pieces and sprinkle with salt and pepper.
2 Put the salmon pieces on a baking sheet and top with the combined
Topping ingredients. Bake in a toaster oven until browned. Cover the
salmon with aluminum foil and bake for another 6 to 7 minutes.

Per serving
174 cal

Cooking time
15 min

Make-Ahead

Keeps in the fridge for
2 days

Keeps in the freezer for
1 month

Microwave Miso Mackerel

No pan required! The key to removing fishy smells is to
pour boiling water over the mackerel before microwaving.

SERVES 1 TO 2

4 oz (100 g) mackerel (saba),
   bluefish or mahi mahi
1 small knob ginger

Sauce
1½ tablespoons miso
1½ tablespoons sugar
1½ tablespoons sake
1½ tablespoons mirin

1 Cut the mackerel in half
lengthwise and cut a cross in
the skin. Put the fish in a colander and pour boiling water over
it. Thinly slice the ginger.

2 Combine the Sauce ingredients in a heatproof bowl.
Add the sliced ginger and fish, skin side down. Cover
with cling film and microwave for 3 to 4 minutes. When
a skewer pierces the fish easily and is warm when
pulled out, it is done.

Per serving
200 cal

Cooking time
10 min

Make-Ahead

Keeps in the fridge for
3 days

Keeps in the freezer for
1 month

Fragrant Miso Swordfish

The ginger and shiso in the sauce are fantastic with steamed rice.

SERVES 1

4 oz (100 g) swordfish
2 slices each lotus root and carrot,
  ¼ inch thick
Salt

Sauce
1 teaspoon miso
1 teaspoon mirin
½ teaspoon grated ginger
1 green shiso or basil leaf, finely minced

1 Combine the Sauce ingredients and spread on the swordfish.
2 Put the fish, lotus root and carrot on a baking sheet and bake 7 to 8 minutes in a toaster oven. Check midway through, and if a skewer easily pierces the lotus root and carrot, remove them.
3 Sprinkle the lotus root and carrot with salt.

Per serving
180 cal

Cooking time
15 min

Make-Ahead

Keeps in the fridge for
2 days

Keeps in the freezer for
1 month

Savory Seafood Pancake

Transfer the frozen seafood for this Korean-style pancake to the refrigerator the day before so you can cook it right away in the morning.

SERVES 3 TO 4

2 oz (50 g) garlic chives
3 oz (80 g) frozen seafood mix
3 tablespoons cornstarch or
  potato starch
2 tablespoons flour
1 egg
1 teaspoon concentrated
  mentsuyu or soy sauce
Salt
2 tablespoons water
1 tablespoon sesame oil

the chives and seafood.
3 Heat the sesame oil in a skillet, pour in the batter and fry over medium heat for about 3 minutes. Flip and cook the other side for about 2 minutes, until cooked through.

1 Roughly chop the garlic chives. Defrost the seafood mix.
2 Combine the starch, flour, egg, mentsuyu or soy sauce, salt and water in a bowl. Mix in

Per serving
103 cal

Cooking time
8 to **10** min

Make-Ahead

Keeps in the fridge for
2 to **3** days

Keeps in the freezer for
1 month

Lesson

Basic Japanese Rolled Omelet

Sweet-and-salty rolled omelets, or tamagoyaki, are a staple of bentos. It takes a little practice to get the technique right, but once you do it's quick and easy. A rectangular pan designed for this purpose and a pair of cooking chopsticks help!

SERVES 2

3 eggs
1 tablespoon sugar
1 teaspoon light soy sauce
Vegetable oil for cooking

Beat the eggs by using a cutting motion with a pair of chopsticks. Try not to create foam.

1

Beat the eggs, add the sugar and soy sauce, and mix.

Once the egg is soft set, start rolling it towards you.

4

Roll the omelet from the far side of the pan to the near side, then tilt the pan to slide the rolled omelet to the back. You can use a spatula for this task.

Always let the pan heat up before you pour in the beaten egg.

2

Heat a small amount of vegetable oil in a rectangular pan over medium-low heat. Pour in ⅓ of the beaten egg. Spread over the bottom of the pan.

When the edges begin to firm up, scramble the eggs.

3

When the egg starts to firm up, stir it quickly with chopsticks to make soft-scrambled eggs.

Lift the rolled egg to let the uncooked egg flow under it.

5

Pour in another ⅓ of the beaten egg, lifting the cooked egg to let the liquid flow under it.

When the omelet has cooled, slice into bite-size pieces and pack in the bento box.

Finished!

6

Repeat Steps 4 and 5, using up the rest of the beaten egg.

Rolled Omelet Variations

Once you've mastered a Basic Rolled Japanese Omelet, you can vary it by adding different seasonings and fillings. Let your creativity be your guide!

Cheesy Rolled Omelet

Wrap a slice of cheese inside to make a pretty spiral.

SERVES 1 TO 2

1 Beat **1 egg**, add a **pinch of salt** and mix.
2 Heat a small amount of **vegetable oil** in a rectangular pan over medium-low heat. Pour in the beaten egg, top with a slice of processed cheese and roll up from one end.
3 When cool, slice into bite-size pieces.

Rolled Omelet with Aonori

Fragrant aonori seaweed permeates this omelet. It is sold powdered, not in sheets like nori.

SERVES 2

1 Beat **2 eggs**, add **½ tablespoon concentrated mentsuyu** (noodle sauce), **1 teaspoon sugar**, and **⅓ teaspoon aonori powder** and mix.
2 Heat a small amount of **vegetable oil** in a rectangular pan over medium-low heat. Follow the steps on pages 66 to 67 to cook the omelet.
3 When cool, slice into bite-size pieces.

Imitation Crab Rolled Omelet

An unusual variation with whole imitation crab sticks inside.

SERVES 2

1 Beat **1 egg**, add a **pinch of salt** and mix.
2 Arrange **4 imitation crab sticks** in pairs and wrap each pair with a quarter of a sheet of **nori**.
3 Heat a small amount of **vegetable oil** in a rectangular pan over medium-low heat. Pour in ½ of the beaten egg, place the wrapped crab sticks crosswise on top and roll up from one edge. Pour in the rest of the egg and roll up again from the edge.
4 When cool, slice into bite-size pieces.

Dried Shrimp Rolled Omelet

Tiny dried shrimp called *sakura ebi* give this omelet a different texture.

SERVES 2

1 Beat **2 eggs**, add **1 tablespoon sakura ebi** (dried shrimp), **2 teaspoons sugar**, and **½ teaspoon light soy sauce** and mix.
2 Heat a small amount of **vegetable oil** in a rectangular pan over medium-low heat. Follow the steps on pages 66 to 67 to cook the omelet, adding the egg in two or three batches.
3 When cool, slice into bite-size pieces.

Lesson

Boiled Eggs with Variations

Carefully place eggs in boiling water and boil for 12 minutes for eggs fresh from the refrigerator and 10 minutes for eggs at room temperature. In the first minute, gently roll the eggs so that the yolk is in the center. Drain, cool in cold water and peel. The boiled eggs can be marinated or baked with toppings to add flavor.

Savory Boiled Eggs

Sweetened soy sauce flavors these eggs.

4 EGGS

1 Put **2 tablespoons soy sauce**, **½ tablespoon sugar**, **1 tablespoon mirin** and **1 tablespoon water** in a small pan. Bring to a boil and let cool. Transfer to a small storage container.
2 Add **4 peeled boiled eggs** and marinate for at least 2 hours and up to 3 days.

Miso Marinated Eggs

The rich flavor of miso goes great with boiled eggs.

4 EGGS

Combine **3 tablespoons miso**, **1 tablespoon mirin** and **1 tablespoon sake** in a bowl. Add **4 peeled boiled eggs** and marinate for at least 2 hours.

Miso-Mayo Eggs

Baking the topped eggs in a toaster oven caramelizes the sauce.

SERVES 1 TO 2

1 Cut **1 peeled boiled egg** in half lengthwise. Combine **1 teaspoon miso** and **1 teaspoon sugar** and spread on the egg halves.
2 Put the eggs on a baking sheet and top with a little **mayonnaise**. Bake in a toaster oven for 3 to 4 minutes.

Cheesy Baked Eggs

Ketchup and cheese make this dish popular with kids.

SERVES 1 TO 2

1 Cut **1 peeled boiled egg** in half lengthwise. Top with a little **ketchup**.
2 Put the egg halves on a baking sheet and top with **shredded pizza cheese**. Bake in a toaster oven for 3 to 4 minutes.
3 When the cheese is lightly browned, top with **dried parsley flakes**.

Cooking with Cocktail Franks

Mini hot dogs and cocktail franks are pre-cooked, so they're very handy for quick recipes.

Stir-Fried Cocktail Franks and Peppers

Adding a vegetable ups the nutrition.

SERVES 1 TO 2

1 Cut **3 cocktail franks** diagonally in half. Seed **1 small bell pepper** and slice thinly.
2 Heat **1 teaspoon vegetable oil** in a small skillet and stir-fry the franks and peppers over medium heat until franks are browned.
3 Drizzle with **½ teaspoon soy sauce** and season with **salt and pepper**.

Mini Corn Dogs

Small enough to fit in a bento box.

SERVES 4 (12 PIECES)

1 Combine **¾ cup (100 g) pancake mix**, **1 egg** and **2 to 3 tablespoons milk** in a medium bowl. Add only enough milk to make a thick batter.
2 Skewer **12 cocktail franks** with tooth-picks. Dip in the batter and deep-fry in 320 °F (160 °C) oil for 3 to 4 minutes, until golden brown. Top with ketchup.

Cheese-Stuffed Cocktail Franks

Homemade cheese sausages!

SERVES 1

1 Cut lengthwise slits in **3 cocktail franks** and stuff with **sliced processed cheese**.
2 Put the stuffed franks on a baking sheet and bake in a toaster oven for 2 to 3 minutes, until the cheese is lightly browned.

SERVES 1 TO 2

Scrambled Eggs and Franks

A quick, high-protein dish.

1 Slice **2 cocktail franks** into rounds. Beat **1 egg**, add **2 teaspoons mayonnaise** and mix.
2 Heat **1 teaspoon vegetable oil** in a small skillet and stir-fry the egg and franks for 1 to 2 minutes. Season with **salt and pepper**.

Part 2
Side Dishes

Red • Yellow • Green • Brown • Black • White

Sides and secondary sides are essential for brightening up your bentos. In this chapter, they're arranged by color to make aesthetic balance easy, and further divided into quick recipes to make in the morning and make-ahead recipes for when you have more time. Choose whatever fits your lifestyle.

My Approach to Sides

Sides and secondary sides add color to bentos, improve overall flavor balance, and boost vitamin and mineral content. On the facing page you'll find some tips for making them quickly and efficiently.

1. Shop for red, yellow and green ingredients

When you're shopping for ingredients for sides, keep color in mind. Choose red and orange foods like cherry tomatoes, red bell peppers and carrots; yellow foods like kabocha squash and corn; and green foods like green bell peppers and broccoli.

2. Less is more when it comes to ingredients

The biggest key to successful sides is to limit yourself to just a few ingredients. This cuts down on chopping and prep time. As a basic rule, try to combine a vegetable in one of the five main color categories with an umami-rich seasoning.

3. Frozen vegetables, dried goods and processed meats are convenient to have on hand

Frozen and boiled vegetables play a huge role in sides and secondary sides. Just add umami-rich ingredients like bonito flakes, dried shrimp or grilled nori; processed meats such as ham, bacon or cocktail franks; or fish-paste products like chikuwa—your options are limitless!

4. Make eggs a bento fixture

Japanese bentos typically include a rolled omelet or boiled egg. They add protein, vitamins, minerals, and yellow color. For rolled omelets, add-ins are any easy way to change up taste and appearance. For boiled eggs, marinating or topping them avoids monotony.

5. Use the microwave and toaster oven so you can cook the main and sides at the same time

Cooking the main and sides at the same time greatly speeds up bento prep. For instance, you can make a side in the microwave while you cook the main in a skillet, or bake both the main and side in a toaster oven.

6. Choose sweet, spicy and sour flavors that go with the main

Once you've decided on a main, use its flavors to determine the side and secondary side. This will ensure a well-balanced bento. Avoid combining a sweet main with a sweet side, for instance. Instead, aim for a balance of sweet, spicy, sour and other flavors.

7. Make big batches of sides that keep well

I recommend making more than one day's worth of marinated and simmered dishes. You can use them for future bentos or even serve them with dinner, making your evening routine easier. For use in bentos, it's convenient to refrigerate or freeze extra servings in silicon cups.

Per serving
101
cal

Cooking time
6 min

Carrots with Tuna and Eggs

This simply seasoned dish from Okinawa, in southern Japan, lets the richness of sesame oil and the sweetness of carrots shine.

SERVES 2

½ **carrot**
½ **can tuna (40 g), drained**
1 teaspoon sesame oil
1 egg, beaten
Salt and pepper

1 Shred the carrot. Drain the liquid from the canned tuna.
2 Heat the sesame oil in a small skillet and stir-fry the carrot for about 1 minute. When it softens, add the tuna and quickly stir-fry together.
3 Add the beaten egg (see photo) and stir-fry together. Season with salt and pepper.

Move the carrot to one side and pour the egg in the empty space.

Carrots with Ketchup

A popular dish with kids.

SERVES 1

1-inch (3-cm) piece carrot
1 slice bacon
1 teaspoon vegetable oil
2 teaspoons ketchup

1 Cut the carrot into wide strips. Thinly slice the bacon.
2 Heat the vegetable oil in a small skillet and stir-fry the carrot and bacon over medium heat for about 1 minute.
3 When the carrot is lightly browned and almost cooked through, add the ketchup and stir-fry to cook off the moisture.

Per serving
139 cal

Cooking time
5 min

Carrots with Spicy Cod Roe

Spicy cod roe (*mentaiko*) is a delicacy that you'll find in the refrigerator section of some Japanese groceries. It adds a fun texture to this dish.

SERVES 2

2-inch (5-cm) piece carrot
¼ sac spicy cod roe (*mentaiko*)
½ tablespoon mayonnaise
Salt and pepper

1 Cut the carrot into strips. Remove the cod roe from its sac.
2 Put the carrot strips in a heatproof bowl, cover with cling film and microwave for 40 seconds. When the carrot is cooked through but still slightly crispy, add the mentaiko, re-cover the bowl with cling film and microwave for another 40 seconds.
3 Mix in the mayonnaise and season with salt and pepper.

Per serving
38 cal

Cooking time
5 min

Ham Wrapped Cherry Tomatoes

Pan-frying the tomatoes makes them sweeter and increases umami!

SERVES 2 (4 PIECES)

4 cherry tomatoes
1 slice ham

1 Cut the ham in 4 strips about the width of the tomatoes.
2 Wrap cherry tomatoes with ham strips and skewer with toothpicks.
3 Heat a skillet and cook the cherry tomatoes, rolling to lightly brown.

Per piece
23 cal

Cooking time
3 min

Honey Lemon Cherry Tomatoes

This refreshing side is nice to nibble between other dishes.

SERVES 2 (6 CHERRY TOMATOES)

6 cherry tomatoes
2 teaspoons lemon juice
2 teaspoons honey
A pinch of salt

1 Cut crosses in the cherry tomatoes.
2 Combine the lemon juice, honey and salt and mix with the tomatoes.

Per piece
11 cal

Cooking time
3 min

Stir-Fried Bell Pepper Rings

Cutting the peppers in rings adds visual interest to this side.

SERVES 1 TO 2

1 small red bell pepper
1 teaspoon olive oil
Pinch of red chili flakes
½ teaspoon soy sauce
½ teaspoon sugar
Toasted white sesame seeds

1 Seed the bell pepper and slice into rounds.
2 Heat the olive oil and chili flakes in a small skillet over low heat. When fragrant, increase the heat to medium, add the pepper rings and stir-fry briefly.
3 When coated in oil, add the soy sauce and sugar and cook for another minute or two. Sprinkle with sesame seeds.

Per serving
67
cal

Cooking time
3 min

Bell Pepper with Honey Mustard

Honey mellows the flavor of the Japanese-style mustard dressing.

SERVES 1

½ red bell pepper

Dressing
½ tablespoon whole grain mustard
½ teaspoon soy sauce
½ teaspoon honey

1 Seed the bell pepper and cut into ½ inch (1.5 cm) squares.
2 Put the bell pepper in a heatproof bowl, cover with cling film and microwave for 50 seconds.
3 If the bell pepper releases moisture, drain it off. Mix the Dressing ingredients and combine with the peppers.

Per serving
46
cal

Cooking time
3 min

Per serving
46 cal

Cooking time
8 min

Keeps in the fridge for
3 days

Keeps in the freezer for
1 month

Quick Ratatouille

Drain the liquid before packing this quick take on the classic French dish.

SERVES 2 TO 4

1 red bell pepper
1 tomato
1 small Asian eggplant
1 tablespoon olive oil
1 teaspoon sugar
1 teaspoon granulated bouillon
Salt and pepper

1 Seed the bell pepper and cut into ½ inch (1.5 cm) squares. Cut the tomato and eggplant into ½ inch (1.5 cm) cubes.
2 Place the vegetables in a heatproof bowl, add the olive oil, sugar, and granulated bouillon and mix (see photo). Cover with cling film and microwave for 4 minutes.
3 When the vegetables have softened, season with salt and pepper.

Just combine the ingredients and microwave!

Sweet and Sour Radishes

These bright red quick pickles work great as gap fillers.

SERVES 5 TO 10 (10 RADISHES)

10 radishes

Marinade
6 tablespoons rice vinegar
2 tablespoons sugar
Pinch of salt
3 tablespoons water

1 Trim the stems off the radishes.
2 Put the Marinade ingredients in a heatproof bowl and microwave for 1 minute. Add the radishes and let marinate at least 3 to 4 hours.

*Excludes pickling time.

Per radish
13 cal

Cooking time
3 min *

Keeps in the fridge for
4–5 days

Marinated Red Onion

Soaking the onion in water removes harshness so it can be enjoyed raw.

SERVES 2 TO 4

1 small red onion

Marinade
3 tablespoons lemon juice
1 tablespoon olive oil
1 teaspoon sugar
Pinch of salt

1 Slice the red onion thinly against the grain and place in a bowl of water for a few minutes. Drain well.
2 Combine the Marinade ingredients in a bowl and add the onion slices. Marinate in the refrigerator for at least an hour.

Per serving
45 cal

Cooking time
3 min

Keeps in the fridge for
3–4 days

Per serving
85 cal

Cooking time
4 min

Spicy Corn, Ham and Bell Pepper Stir-Fry

Chili flakes add a kick to the sweet ingredients in this dish. You may want to omit them if you're cooking for young kids.

SERVES 1

¼ yellow bell pepper
1 slice ham
1 teaspoon olive oil
Pinch of red chili flakes
2 tablespoons canned or frozen whole corn kernels
Salt and pepper

1 Seed and thinly slice the bell pepper. Thinly slice the ham.
2 Heat the olive oil with the chili flakes in a small skillet and stir-fry the peppers, ham, and corn briefly.
3 When the oil has coated the ingredients, remove from heat and season with salt and pepper.

Stir-fry just long enough to coat the veggies and ham with oil.

Corn & Egg Salad

Kids tend to like this simple, creamy salad.

SERVES 2

1 hardboiled egg, peeled
2 tablespoons frozen or canned whole corn
  kernels
2 tablespoons mayonnaise
½ teaspoon rice vinegar
Salt and pepper

1 Chop the boiled egg.
2 Combine the egg with the corn, mayonnaise
and vinegar in a small bowl. Season with salt
and pepper.

Per serving
129
cal

Cooking time
2 min

Cheesy Corn Rounds

Since the cheese is salty, there's no need
to add seasonings.

SERVES 2

2 tablespoons canned or frozen whole corn kernels
1 oz (30 g) shredded pizza cheese

1 Put the corn kernels on a paper towel and pat dry.
2 Sprinkle the shredded cheese in 1 inch (3 cm)
circles on a skillet. Turn on the burner to medium and
top with the corn.
3 When the cheese starts to melt, flip the patties and
cook on the other side for a few minutes. Cool on a
piece of parchment paper.

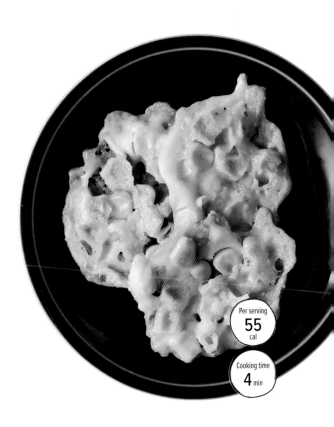

Per serving
55
cal

Cooking time
4 min

Curried Squash Crescents

Butternut, acorn, and kabocha squash all work well in this recipe.

SERVES 2

2 oz (50 g) kabocha or other winter squash, seeded
2 teaspoons olive oil
2 to 3 pinches curry powder
Salt and pepper

1 Slice the squash into thin crescents.
2 Heat the olive oil in a medium skillet and cook the squash over medium heat for a minute on each side.
3 When the squash is cooked through, sprinkle on the curry powder and season with salt and pepper.

Per serving
46 cal

Cooking time
3 min

Winter Squash with Sesame

The nutty flavor of sesame goes great with sweet winter squash. Buy ground sesame seeds or toast and grind your own in a mortar and pestle.

SERVES 2

4 oz (100 g) kabocha, butternut or acorn squash, seeded
½ teaspoon concentrated mentsuyu or soy sauce
1 tablespoon ground sesame seeds

1 Cut the squash into bite-size pieces. Place in a heatproof bowl, cover with cling film and microwave for 1 minute. If not tender, microwave for another 20 seconds.
2 When tender, mix with the mentsuyu or soy sauce and ground sesame seeds.

Per serving
41 cal

Cooking time
4 min

Bell Pepper and Fishcake Bundles

This ultra easy side doesn't need to be cooked or seasoned.

SERVES 1

⅙ yellow bell pepper
1 piece chikuwa (tube-shaped fishcake)
1 slice processed cheese

1 Slice the chikuwa into ½ inch (1.5 cm) rings. Seed the bell pepper and thinly slice. Thinly slice the cheese.
2 Stuff the bell pepper and cheese into the chikuwa ring holes.

*In the summer or any time food poisoning is a concern, cook the stuffed rings in a skillet with a little oil over medium heat, rolling to lightly brown on all sides.

Per serving
71 cal

Cooking time
2 min

Baby Corn and Cheese

A simple, super quick side.

SERVES 1 TO 2

5 to 6 canned baby corns
1 teaspoon grated cheese
1 teaspoon olive oil
Salt

1 Heat the olive oil in a small skillet and stir-fry the baby corn for about 1 minute.
2 When it is lightly browned, sprinkle with the grated cheese and season with salt.

Per serving
30 cal

Cooking time
2 min

Per piece
64 cal

Cooking time
12 min

Keeps in
the fridge for
2–3 days

Keeps in the
freezer for
1 month

Mini Squash Croquettes

Butter gives these croquettes a pleasant fragrance and flavor.

SERVES 4 TO 6 (12 CROQUETTES)

¼ kabocha, butternut or acorn squash (about **14 oz/400 g**), seeded and peeled
1 tablespoon butter
1 teaspoon soy sauce
1 teaspoon sugar
Salt and pepper
Flour for dusting
1 egg, beaten
Panko breadcrumbs
Vegetable oil for frying

1 Cut the squash into bite-size pieces. Place in a heatproof bowl, cover with cling film and microwave for 3 minutes.

2 When the kabocha squash is tender, mash it with the butter, soy sauce, salt and pepper. Divide into 12 portions and form into balls (see photo). Coat with flour, beaten egg and breadcrumbs in that order.

3 Heat about 1 inch (2.5 cm) of oil in a skillet to 355 °F (180 °C; see Tip page 42). Fry the croquettes until golden brown, about 3 to 4 minutes.

These bite-size balls fit easily in a bento box.

Curried Baby Onion Pickles

The natural sweetness of onions shines in this recipe.

SERVES 3 TO 6 (6 ONIONS)

6 small onions

Marinade
6 tablespoons rice vinegar
2 teaspoons concentrated mentsuyu or soy sauce
1 teaspoon curry powder
3 tablespoons water

1 Put the onions in a heatproof bowl, cover with cling film and microwave for 2 minutes or until a skewer easily pierces them.
2 Add the Marinade ingredients to the onions, cover with cling film and microwave for another minute. Let cool.

Per piece
21 cal

Cooking time
6 min

Keeps in the fridge for
7 days

Glazed Sweet Potato Chunks

Try to find Japanese sweet potatoes for this recipe. They have dry, pale flesh and maroon skin.

SERVES 6 TO 8

1 large Japanese sweet potato (about 1 lb/500 g)
Vegetable oil for frying
1½ tablespoons sugar
1½ tablespoons mirin
1 teaspoon light soy sauce
Toasted black sesame seeds

1 Cut the sweet potato into rough chunks with the skin on.
2 Heat about 1 inch (2.5 cm) of oil in a deep skillet to 355 °F (180 °C; see Tip page 42). Fry the sweet potato for 4 to 5 minutes, until easily pierced by a skewer.
3 In another skillet, heat the sugar, mirin and soy sauce over medium heat. When the mixture comes to a boil, add the fried sweet potatoes and stir to coat. Sprinkle with the sesame seeds.
4 Spread the potatoes on parchment paper so that the pieces are not touching. Let cool.

Per serving
112 cal

Cooking time
8 min

Keeps in the fridge for
2–3 days

Keeps in the freezer for
1 month

Per serving
45 cal

Cooking time
4 min

Sesame-Miso Green Beans

Miso gives unexpected depth to this simple dish. Buy ground sesame seeds or toast and grind your own in a mortar and pestle.

Pat the green beans dry so they don't make the sauce watery.

SERVES 1 TO 2

10 green beans
Salt

Dressing
1 tablespoon ground white sesame seeds
1 teaspoon miso
1 teaspoon sugar
¼ teaspoon soy sauce

1 Boil the green beans in salted water for about 2 minutes. Cut into 1-inch (2- to 3-cm) pieces and pat dry.
2 Combine the Dressing ingredients in a small bowl and toss with the green beans (see photo).

VARIATION:

Sugar Snap Peas with Walnuts and Miso

Remove the strings from **8 sugar snap peas** and boil in salted water for about 90 seconds. Mix with **1 teaspoon miso, 1 teaspoon sugar, ½ teaspoon mirin** and **1 tablespoon chopped walnuts**.

Stir-Fried Peppers With Tiny Fish

For this recipe, look for triple-concentrated mentsuyu (noodle sauce) or substitute soy sauce—though mentsuyu has a sweeter, more complex flavor.

SERVES 1 TO 2

1 small green bell pepper
1 tablespoon dried baby anchovies (*chirimen jako*)
½ teaspoon concentrated mentsuyu
1 teaspoon vegetable oil

1 Seed and thinly slice the bell pepper.
2 Heat the oil in a small skillet and cook the pepper slices over medium heat for 30 to 40 seconds.
3 When the oil has coated the peppers, add the dried anchovies and mentsuyu and stir-fry briefly.

Per serving
31 cal

Cooking time
3 min

Baked Asparagus with Peppery Cheese

The salty, spicy topping highlights the sweetness of the asparagus.

SERVES 1 TO 3

3 asparagus spears
2 teaspoons grated cheese
Salt and coarsely ground black pepper

1 Remove the tough root ends from the asparagus and cut the spears into 1½-inch (4-cm) lengths.
2 Skewer 3 or 4 of the pieces together with 2 toothpicks. Repeat with the remaining pieces.
3 Place the asparagus on a baking sheet, sprinkle with grated cheese, salt and pepper, and bake in a toaster oven for 4 to 5 minutes, or until the grated cheese is browned.

Per piece
9 cal

Cooking time
8 min

Sesame Shishito Peppers

A simple recipe that can be made in any quantity you want. If you can't find shishito peppers, try substituting padrons or small banana peppers.

SERVES 2

½ tablespoon vegetable oil
8 shishito peppers
Salt
Toasted white sesame seeds

1 Heat the oil in a small skillet and stir-fry the peppers over medium heat for about 1 minute.
2 When they are lightly browned, sprinkle with salt and sesame seeds and stir-fry to combine.

Per serving
38
cal

Cooking time
2 min

Simple Blanched Greens

Komatsuna is a mild, quick-cooking Japanese green. The same technique works well with other mild, tender greens like spinach, bok choy, or chard.

SERVES 1 TO 2

3 oz (90 g) komatsuna greens
Bonito flakes
Soy sauce

1 Boil the komatsuna greens for about 1 minute. Drain and cool under running water. Squeeze firmly to remove excess moisture and cut into 1-inch (3-cm) lengths.
2 Top with katsuobushi and soy sauce to taste.

Per serving
6
cal

Cooking time
3 min

Cucumber and Cottage Cheese Salad

A refreshing, simple and healthy salad.

SERVES 2

1 small cucumber
Salt

Dressing
2 tablespoons cottage cheese
Salt and pepper
1 teaspoon olive oil

1 Peel strips off the cucumber and slice into rounds. Sprinkle with salt and massage, squeezing to remove excess moisture.
2 Combine the Dressing ingredients in a small bowl and add the cucumber.

Per serving
39 cal

Cooking time
2 min

Okra with Smoky Fish Flakes

Okra has little moisture, making it a great choice for bentos. Prepared this way, it's not overly slimy.

SERVES 2

4 to 5 okra
Salt
Large pinch bonito flakes
½ teaspoon toasted white sesame seeds
½ teaspoon soy sauce

1 Rub the okra firmly on a cutting board to remove the surface hairs. Boil for 1 minute, drain, and transfer to a bowl of ice water. Drain well and cut in half diagonally.
2 Sprinkle with bonito flakes, sesame seeds and soy sauce.

Per serving
14 cal

Cooking time
3 min

Per serving
87 cal

Cooking time
5 min

Keeps in the fridge for
3–4 days

Broccoli and Egg Salad

Drain the boiled broccoli thoroughly before adding the other ingredients.

SERVES 4 TO 6

1 head of broccoli
2 hardboiled eggs, peeled
4 tablespoons mayonnaise
Salt and pepper

1 Divide the broccoli into small florets, boil in salted water for about 2 minutes, and drain well. Roughly chop the eggs (see photo).
2 Combine the broccoli, egg, and mayonnaise. Season with salt and pepper.

The chopped egg clings to the broccoli like a dressing.

Sesame Spinach

This Korean-style side is packed with sesame seeds. It's addictively delicious.

SERVES 4 TO 5

7 oz (200 g) spinach
Salt

Dressing
1 tablespoon ground white sesame seeds
1 teaspoon granulated chicken bouillon
1 teaspoon sesame oil

1 Boil the spinach in salted water for about 1 minute, drain, and cool under running water. Squeeze firmly to remove excess moisture and cut into 1-inch (2- to 3-cm) lengths.
2 Mix the spinach with the Dressing ingredients.

Per serving
23
cal

Cooking time
3 min

Keeps in the fridge for
3–4 days

Keeps in the freezer for
1 month

Cabbage-Edamame Slaw

The edamame add a nice textural accent to this refreshing salad.

SERVES 4 TO 6

¼ cabbage (about 8 oz/250 g)
¼ onion
4 tablespoons shelled cooked edamame
Salt and pepper

Dressing
1 tablespoon mayonnaise
1 teaspoon rice vinegar

1 Shred the cabbage and massage with a pinch of salt. Squeeze firmly to remove excess moisture. Thinly slice the onion and massage with a pinch of salt, then rinse under running water and squeeze to remove moisture.
2 Combine the onion, cabbage and edamame with the Dressing ingredients. Season with salt and pepper.

Per serving
37
cal

Cooking time
5 min

Keeps in the fridge for
3–4 days

Per serving
102 cal

Cooking time
5 min

Fried Tofu "Pizzas"

This satisfying dish uses thin sheets of deep-fried tofu available in Asian grocery stores as a base for a miso and cheese topping.

SERVES 1 TO 2

1 sheet aburaage (fried tofu)
3 tablespoons shredded pizza cheese

Topping
2 teaspoons minced green onion
1 teaspoon miso
½ teaspoon sugar
½ teaspoon mirin

1 Combine the Topping ingredients and spread on the aburaage (see photo). Cut into 4 triangles.
2 Put the triangles on a baking sheet, top with cheese and bake in the toaster oven for 2 to 3 minutes, until the cheese is browned.

Use the back of a spoon to spread the miso mixture.

VARIATION:

Fried Tofu "Pizzas" with Pickles

Cut **1 sheet aburaage** in quarters. Top with **1 tablespoon minced Japanese pickles**, such as mustard greens or daikon, and **3 tablespoons shredded pizza cheese**. Bake in a toaster oven for 3 to 4 minutes until the cheese is browned.

Microwave Simmered Vegetables

Look for strips of dried daikon radish, called kiriboshi daikon, in an Asian grocery store. Rehydrate it the night before for an easy morning.

Per serving
86 cal

Cooking time
8 min

SERVES 2

½ oz (15 g) kiriboshi daikon
1 fried fishcake (satsuma-age)
1-inch (2-cm) piece carrot

Sauce
2 teaspoons soy sauce
2 teaspoons mirin
2 teaspoons sugar
Large pinch bonito flakes
3 tablespoons water

1 Rehydrate the kiriboshi daikon in cold water according to package instructions. Cut the fishcake and carrot into thin strips.
2 Put the kiriboshi daikon, fishcake, carrot and Sauce ingredients in a heatproof bowl, cover with cling film and microwave for 3 to 4 minutes, until seasonings permeate ingredients.

Fishcake Tempura

Fragrant aonori seaweed makes this batter delicious even when cold. Tempura mix is handy for making the small amount of batter called for.

SERVES 2

2 pieces tube-shaped fishcake (chikuwa)
Vegetable oil for frying

Batter
1 tablespoon tempura mix
1 tablespoon water
¼ teaspoon aonori powder (ground seaweed)

Per serving
202 cal

Cooking time
5 min

1 Combine the Batter ingredients. Dip the chikuwa in it to coat.
2 Heat about ¾ inch (2 cm) of oil in a small skillet to 355 °F (180 °C; see Tip page 42). Fry until the chikuwa is golden brown, about 2 minutes. Cut into bite-size pieces.

Spicy Eggplant Wedges

The heat in this recipe comes from doubanjiang, a spicy Chinese bean paste. It's tasty with steamed rice.

SERVES 1 TO 2

1 small Asian eggplant
2 teaspoons vegetable oil
½ teaspoon doubanjiang (spicy Chinese bean paste)
1 teaspoon soy sauce

1 Cut the eggplant lengthwise into 6 equal pieces. Cut each piece in half or quarters lengthwise.
2 Heat the vegetable oil in a medium skillet and cook the eggplant for about 2 minutes over medium heat.
3 When the eggplant softens, add the doubanjiang and soy sauce and mix.

Per serving
46 cal

Cooking time
5 min

Eggplant with Black Sesame

Eggplant soaks up oil when fried and can become greasy. Microwaving it with just a little oil solves the problem.

SERVES 1 TO 2

1 small Asian eggplant
1 teaspoon vegetable oil
Salt

Dressing
2 teaspoons ground black sesame seeds
½ teaspoon soy sauce
½ teaspoon sugar

1 Cut the eggplant into large chunks and place in a heatproof bowl. Drizzle with the oil. Cover the bowl with cling film and micro-wave for 90 seconds.
2 When the eggplant has softened, mix with the Dressing ingredients. Season with salt.

Per serving
41 cal

Cooking time
4 min

Baked Miso-Mayo Shiitake Mushrooms

Mayonnaise in a squirt bottle works well for this recipe.

SERVES 1

2 shiitake mushrooms
½ teaspoon miso
Mayonnaise

1 Remove the stems from the shiitake mushrooms and spread the insides of the caps with miso.
2 Place the shiitake mushroom caps on a baking sheet and squeeze a zigzag of mayonnaise on each. Bake in a toaster oven for 3 to 4 minutes until browned.

Per serving
47 cal

Cooking time
6 min

Maitake Mushrooms with Citrusy Butter Sauce

Store-bought ponzu sauce is a great time-saver. It's tasty with other kinds of mushrooms, too.

SERVES 2

4 oz (100 g) maitake mushrooms
**   (hen of the woods)**
2 teaspoons butter
1 tablespoon ponzu sauce
Salt and pepper

1 Trim the tough stem ends off the mushrooms and divide into small clumps.
2 Heat the butter in a medium skillet and stir-fry the maitake mushrooms for 1 to 2 minutes over medium heat.
3 When the butter has coated the mushrooms, add the ponzu sauce and simmer until the liquid is gone. Season with salt and pepper.

Per serving
52 cal

Cooking time
4 min

Per serving
120
cal

Cooking time
20 min

Keeps in the fridge for
4–5 days

Keeps in the freezer for
1 month *

Chicken with Japanese Root Vegetables

This is classic Japanese comfort food. If you can't find the Japanese vegetables, try substituting carrots, boiling potatoes and turnips.

SERVES 4 TO 6

6 cooked taro roots, about 7 oz (200 g) total; see Note
4-inch (10-cm) piece lotus root
1 piece konnyaku, about 7 oz (200 g)
5 oz (150 g) boneless chicken thigh
1 tablespoon sesame oil

Simmering Liquid
1½ tablespoons soy sauce
1½ tablespoons sugar
1½ tablespoons sake
1½ tablespoons mirin
½ tablespoon concentrated mentsuyu or additional soy sauce
⅔ cup (150 ml) water

1 Cut the taro roots into bite-size pieces if they are large. Halve the lotus root lengthwise and thinly slice. Cut the konnyaku into bite-size pieces with a spoon. Cut the chicken into small pieces.

2 Heat the sesame oil in a medium skillet and stir-fry the vegetables and chicken for about 2 minutes over medium heat. When the oil has coated the ingredients add the Simmering Liquid ingredients (see photo), cover the pan and simmer for about 10 minutes. Stir occasionally. When tender, remove lid and reduce liquid slightly.

*Konnyaku does not freeze well, so omit if freezing.

Add the seasonings after the oil has coated the ingredients.

NOTE: Vacuum-packed pre-cooked taro roots may be available at an Asian grocery store. If not, scrub about 6 unpeeled Japanese taro roots, score around the middle with a knife, and place in a heatproof bowl. Drizzle with a few tablespoons of water, cover loosely with cling film and microwave for 4 to 5 minutes until easily pierced by a skewer. Peel while warm.

Burdock Root Kinpira

Kinpira is a type of spicy, crunchy stir-fry. It's a standard Japanese side dish that's handy for adding textural contrast to bentos.

SERVES 4 TO 6

1 thin burdock root or carrot, about 5 oz (150 g)
1 tablespoon sesame oil
Toasted white sesame seeds

Sauce
1 dried red chili pepper, seeded and
   sliced into rounds
2 teaspoons soy sauce
2 teaspoons sake
2 teaspoons sugar
2 teaspoons mirin

1 Cut the burdock root into thin sticks.
2 Heat the sesame oil in a medium skillet and stir-fry the burdock over medium heat for 2 to 3 minutes.
3 When the burdock softens, add the Sauce ingredients and stir-fry until the moisture is gone. Sprinkle with sesame seeds.

Per serving
46 cal

Cooking time
8 min

Keeps in the fridge for
3–4 days

Keeps in the freezer for
1 month

Simmered Hijiki Seaweed

Glossy black hijiki adds a strong accent to the colors of a bento. Find it in Asian grocery stores or online.

SERVES 4 TO 6

½ oz (15 g) dried hijiki
1 sheet aburaage (thin fried tofu)
¼ carrot
4 tablespoons canned soybeans
1 tablespoon sesame oil

Simmering Liquid
1 tablespoon soy sauce
1 tablespoon sugar
1 tablespoon mirin
1 tablespoon sake

1 Soak the hijiki in cold water to rehydrate. Drain well. Cut the aburaage and carrot into thin strips.
2 Heat the sesame oil in a medium skillet and stir-fry the carrot for about 1 minute. Add the hijiki and aburaage and stir-fry briefly.
3 Add the soybeans and Simmering Liquid ingredients and simmer until the moisture is gone.

Per serving
82 cal

Cooking time
8 min

Keeps in the fridge for
3–4 days

Keeps in the freezer for
1 month

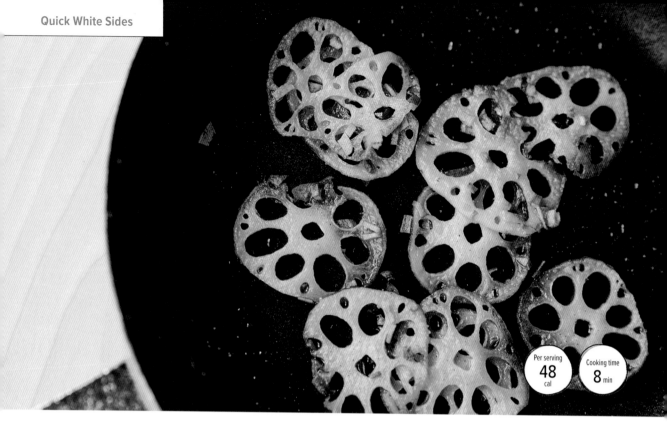

Per serving
48
cal

Cooking time
8 min

Spicy Lotus Root

This nutty, crispy lotus root is spiked with red chili pepper and garlic.

SERVES 1 TO 2

1-inch (3-cm) piece lotus root or medium boiling potato
⅓ garlic clove
⅓ dried red chili pepper
2 teaspoons olive oil
Salt and pepper

1 Slice the lotus root about ⅛ inch (3 mm) thick. Mince the garlic. Seed the red chili pepper and slice into rounds.

2 Heat the olive oil and garlic in a medium skillet over low heat. When the oil is fragrant, raise the heat to medium, add the lotus root and chili pepper and stir-fry for 1 to 2 minutes.

3 When the lotus root is cooked through (see photo), season with salt and pepper.

The lotus root is cooked through when the slices are translucent.

Potato Salad

A microwave makes quick work of cooking the vegetables for this dish.

Per serving
122 cal

Cooking time
10 min

SERVES 4 TO 6

1 potato
1-inch (2-cm) piece carrot
¼ small cucumber
1 slice ham
2 tablespoons mayonnaise
Salt and pepper

1 Quarter the carrot lengthwise and slice. Place in a heatproof bowl, sprinkle with 1 tablespoon of water, cover with cling film and microwave for 40 to 50 seconds, until softened. Slice the cucumber and massage with a pinch of salt. Squeeze to remove excess moisture. Slice the ham thinly.
2 Wash the potato, wrap with a moistened paper towel, then wrap with cling film. Microwave for 3 to 4 minutes, until easily pierced with a skewer.

3 Peel and crush the potato. Mix with the carrot, cucumber, ham and mayonnaise while still hot. Season with salt and pepper.

*During summer or any time food poisoning is a concern, pour boiling water over the sliced ham, or cover with cling film and microwave for 20 to 30 seconds.

Cauliflower with Cottage Cheese

A mild, pure–white side dish.

SERVES 1 TO 2

5 to 6 cauliflower florets, about 3 oz (80 g)
2 tablespoons cottage cheese
Salt and pepper

1 Divide the cauliflower into small florets and boil in salted water until just tender, about 3 minutes. Drain.
2 Mix with the cottage cheese, salt and pepper.

Per serving
17 cal

Cooking time
6 min

Turnip and Kombu Salad

The preserved kombu strips called shio kombu add both saltiness and umami to this easy side. Make sure to use a tender salad turnip.

SERVES 2

1 small salad turnip
Salt
Large pinch shio kombu

1 Cut the turnip in half lengthwise, then crosswise into ⅕ inch (5 mm) slices. Massage with a pinch of salt. Squeeze firmly to remove excess moisture.
2 Add the shio kombu and massage to combine.

Per serving
12
cal

Cooking time
3 min

Crunchy Shredded Daikon Radish

Simple but crunchy and irresistible.

SERVES 2

1-inch (2-cm) piece daikon radish
Salt
⅓ teaspoon sesame oil
Coarsely ground black pepper

1 Cut the daikon into thin strips using a mandoline. Massage with salt and squeeze to remove excess moisture.
2 Drizzle with sesame oil and coarsely ground black pepper.

Per serving
10
cal

Cooking time
4 min

Butter Fried Straw Mushrooms

Butter gives this dish a rich flavor.

SERVES 2

4 oz (100 g) straw (enoki) mushrooms
2 teaspoons butter
Salt

1 Remove the tough bottoms of the mushrooms and cut in half.
2 Heat the butter in a small skillet and stir-fry the mushrooms over medium heat until wilted. Season with salt.

Per serving
53 cal

Cooking time
3 min

Celery Salad with Sesame

Slicing the celery paper thin makes all the difference in this Chinese-style salad.

SERVES 2

½ celery stalk, about 2 oz (50 g)
½ teaspoon granulated chicken bouillon
¼ dried red chili pepper, seeded and cut into rings, optional
⅓ teaspoon sesame oil

1 Remove the tough strings from the celery and slice very thinly.
2 Mix with the granulated bouillon, chili rings if using, and sesame oil.

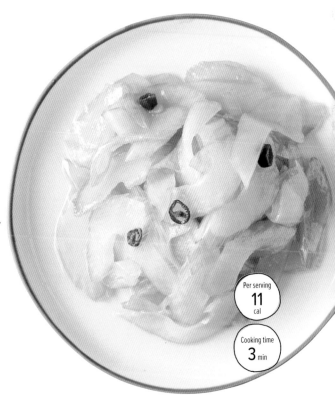

Per serving
11 cal

Cooking time
3 min

Per serving
64 cal

Cooking time
12 min

Keeps in the fridge for
3–4 days

Keeps in the freezer for*
1 month

Creamy Mashed Potatoes

Creamy Mashed Potatoes make for an unconventional but tasty bento side.

SERVES 4 TO 6

3 small potatoes, about 10 oz (300 g) total
½ cup (100 ml) milk
1 tablespoon + 1 teaspoon butter
Salt and pepper

1 Peel the potatoes and cut into bite-size pieces. Boil in just enough water to cover for 4 to 5 minutes, until easily pierced by a skewer.

2 Drain well and mash the potatoes in the pot.

3 Add the milk and butter and cook briefly over medium heat (see photo). Season with salt and pepper.

Mashing the potatoes in the pan saves a bowl.

Bean Sprouts with Tuna

A refreshing salad with an oil and vinegar dressing.

SERVES 3 TO 4

7 oz (200 g) bean sprouts
Scant ½ cup tuna, drained (about 3 oz/80 g)
½ tablespoon rice vinegar
½ tablespoon olive oil
Salt and pepper

1 In a medium saucepan, boil the bean sprouts for 1 minute. Drain well.
2 Mix the bean sprouts with the tuna, rice vinegar and olive oil. Season with salt and pepper.

Per serving
75 cal

Cooking time
3 min

Keeps in the fridge for
2–3 days

Sweet and Sour Napa Cabbage

This quick pickle has the perfect balance of sweetness and spice.

SERVES 4 TO 6

3 napa cabbage leaves (about 8 oz/250 g)
½ teaspoon salt

Dressing
2 tablespoons rice vinegar
1 tablespoon sugar
1 dried red chili pepper, seeded and cut in rings

1 Slice the stems of the cabbage leaves ⅓ inch (1 cm) wide. Roughly chop the leafy parts.
2 Combine the Dressing ingredients in a bowl, add the cabbage and marinate for at least 10 minutes.

*Does not include marinating time.

Per serving
13 cal

Cooking time
4 min

Keeps in the fridge for
4–5 days

Lesson
Cute Sides for Happy Kids

Adding just one of these cute sides makes a child's bento instantly more appealing.

Egg Flowers

Shape the eggs while still hot to form the petals.

Use bamboo skewers and cling film to shape the eggs.

2 EGGS

1 Spread a piece of cling film 20 inches (50 cm) long on the counter and place **2 hot, freshly boiled eggs** side by side on the end closest to you. Wrap the cling film around them once.
2 Place 5 bamboo skewers at ¾ inch (2 cm) intervals on the remaining cling film. Roll the eggs away from you so that the cling wrap holds the skewers tightly against the eggs.
3 Adjust the position of the bamboo skewers so they are evenly spaced. Leave until the eggs are cool (see photo).
4 Remove the cling film and bamboo skewers and cut the eggs in half.

Quail Eggs in Pepper Rings

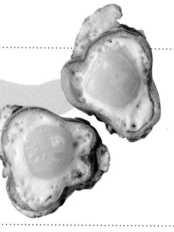

Small Japanese peppers are just right for quail eggs. For Western bell peppers, use chicken eggs.

2 EGGS

1 Heat **1 teaspoon of vegetable oil** in a small skillet. Slice **1 Japanese green pepper** ⅕ inch (5 mm) wide and put 2 slices in the skillet.
2 Break **2 quail eggs** into the pepper slices and cook for 1 to 2 minutes over medium heat.
3 When the eggs are cooked through, season with **salt**.

Ham and Cheese Spirals

The spiral pattern draws the eye.

SERVES 1

Place **1 slice of processed cheese** on top of **1 slice of ham** and roll up tightly from one end. Cut into bite-size pieces.

* In summer or any time food poisoning is a concern, coat the rolls in flour, dip in beaten egg and panko breadcrumbs, and fry until golden brown in 355 °F (180 °C) oil.

Baloney Flower

All it takes is a single slice of deli meat to add cuteness!

SERVES 1

Fold **1 slice of baloney** in half and make cuts ⅛ inch (3 mm) apart on the folded side. Roll the ham up from one edge and secure with a toothpick.

* In summer or any time food poisoning is a concern, place the baloney flower on a piece of aluminum foil on a baking sheet and bake in a toaster oven for 2 to 3 minutes. The flower will be less fluffy when cooked.

Part 3

Rice, Noodles & Bread

Switching out plain steamed rice for flavored rice, noodles, or sandwiches opens up endless options for your bentos. In this chapter, you'll find all of that plus ideas for thermos bentos and lessons on making rice balls and sandwiches.

My Approach to Starches

Steamed white rice is the most common main starch in a bento, but pasta and bread aren't off limits. Getting creative will keep bento eaters from getting bored. Vary the toppings, too.

1. Steamed rice is your go-to bento carb, but try noodles and bread sometimes, too

Rice is the basic main starch for a bento, with variations ranging from rice balls to fried rice. Noodle dishes like pasta and yakisoba are also great because you can load them with veggies and protein. Sandwiches are also an option.

2. Keep a few easy toppings for rice on hand

Plain steamed rice looks a little boring in a bento box. Adding a classic Japanese topping like salty tsukudani preserves, Japanese pickles, shio kombu strips, sesame seeds, or furikake flakes is an easy way to boost flavor and visual interest. Keep a good selection of these in your pantry and fridge.

3. Stock up on spaghetti, fresh ramen noodles, and frozen udon noodles

These all work well in bentos and come in handy if you happen to run out of rice. Fresh ramen noodles can be frozen either raw or pre-steamed. If you include plenty of meat or seafood and vegetables in a noodle dish, you only need to add one or two small sides.

4. Thermoses are great for stews and curries

For bentos based around a stew, curry or hearty soup, a thermos is essential. For a curry bento, for instance, simply ladle your piping hot curry into the thermos, pack a separate bento box with steamed rice and a small side, and you're done. Rice balls and bread both work nicely with soups.

5. Wrap rice balls and sandwiches in cling film

Rice balls and sandwiches are heavy hitters in bentos. Depending on the filling, they can be a satisfying dish all on their own. Another plus is that they can be wrapped in cling film and thrown in your bag, skipping the bento box altogether.

6. Pack more carbs for growing kids, active teenagers, and adults with physical jobs

Increase the serving size of the main starch to be sure growing kids and those who play sports or have physically demanding jobs get enough calories. Refer to pages 26 and 32 through 35 for serving size guidelines for rice. For noodle dishes and sandwiches, increase serving sizes by about 1.5.

7. Use antimicrobial foods like pickled plums to prevent spoilage

Adding 1 pickled plum (umeboshi) to the pot when you cook 2 cups of rice helps prevent the rice from spoiling in the bento box. You can remove and discard the pickled plum before packing the rice, or you can chop it up and mix into the rice for more flavor and color. Adding 1 teaspoon of vinegar when cooking rice has a similar effect. Alternately, mix chopped green shiso leaves or finely minced ginger into cooked white rice.

Curry in a Thermos Bento

A small thermos that can keep food warm or cold and doesn't pose a risk of leaks is the key to expanding your bento repertoire even further. Japanese-style stew and curry are good places to start. Pick up the curry roux cubes at an Asian grocery store. While you're there, search for *fukujinzuke*, a mixed pickle that is the classic accompaniment to Japanese curry.

Boiled sugar snap peas

Cheesy Rolled Omelet
▶ Page 68

Kiwi

Per serving
714
cal

Cooking time
25 min

* Does not include calories or cooking time for sides and fruit.

FOR A 1¼ CUP (300 ML) THERMOS

2 oz (60 g) pork shoulder, cubed
Salt and pepper
¼ onion
⅓ carrot
1 small potato
2 teaspoons vegetable oil
Scant 1 cup (200 ml) water
1 block Japanese curry roux, about ⅔ oz (20 g)
About 1 cup (200 g) cooked white rice
Fukujinzuke or other Japanese pickles

1 Season the pork with salt and pepper. Thinly slice the onion. Roughly chop the carrot and cut the potato into bite-size pieces.
2 Heat the vegetable oil in a medium skillet and stir-fry the pork over medium heat for about 1 minute. When the meat changes color, add the vegetables and continue stir-frying until the oil coats all the ingredients. Add the water, cover the pan and simmer for 10 to 12 minutes.
3 When the vegetables are cooked through, reduce heat to low, add the curry roux and simmer, stirring, until dissolved and thickened, about 3 to 4 minutes.
4 Ladle the curry into a thermos. Pack the rice and pickles into a separate container.

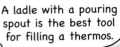

A ladle with a pouring spout is the best tool for filling a thermos.

VARIATION:

Chicken Stew in a Thermos Bento
A mild, comforting dish that's perfect for cold weather.

FOR A 1¼ CUP (300-ML) THERMOS

3 oz (80 g) boneless chicken thigh
1 small potato
⅓ carrot
½ onion
3 to 4 green beans
1½ teaspoons butter
1 tablespoon flour
1 teaspoon granulated bouillon
⅔ cup (150 ml) water
Scant 1 cup (200 ml) milk
3 tablespoons heavy cream (optional)
Salt and pepper

* To keep foods hot longer, pre-heat the thermos by pouring boiling water into it and draining before filling.

1 Cut the chicken into bite-size pieces and sprinkle with salt and pepper. Quarter the potato and roughly chop the carrot. Cut the onion into wedges. Top and tail the green beans and cut in half.
2 Heat the butter in a pan and stir-fry the chicken over medium heat for 1 to 2 minutes. When the meat changes color, add the vegetables and continue stir-frying to coat all ingredients with butter. Sprinkle with flour, add the water and granulated bouillon and cover the pan. Simmer over low heat for 10 to 12 minutes, stirring occasionally.
3 When the vegetables are cooked through, add the milk and simmer for 3 to 4 minutes. When thickened, add the cream, if using, bring to a boil, and season with salt and pepper.

Broccoli and Egg Salad (page 90) and steamed rice round out the meal.

Per serving
688 cal

Cooking time
25 min

Thai Basil Chicken Bento

Packing this bento is easy—just pile everything on the rice. This is a simple take on Pad Krapow Gai, a Thai dish made with fish sauce and fresh basil.

Creamy Mashed Potatoes
▶ Page 102

Per serving
704
cal

Cooking time
12 min

* Does not include calories or cooking time for the Creamy Mashed Potatoes.

SERVES 1

2 teaspoons vegetable oil
1 egg
3 to 4 small broccoli florets
½ dried red chili pepper, seeded and sliced into rounds
¼ onion, chopped
4 oz (100 g) ground chicken
1 small green bell pepper, cut into small squares
½ red bell pepper, cut into small squares
6 to 7 basil leaves, torn
About 1 cup (200 g) cooked rice

Sauce
2 teaspoons sake
1 teaspoon Thai fish sauce (nam pla)
1 teaspoon oyster sauce
½ teaspoon sugar
½ clove garlic

1 Heat 1 teaspoon of the vegetable oil in a skillet, break in the egg and cook over medium heat for about 3 minutes. Add the broccoli on one side, cover the pan and cook over low heat for about 3 minutes. Remove both from the skillet.
2 Wipe out the skillet and add the remaining 1 teaspoon of oil. Stir-fry the red chili pepper and onion over medium heat for about 1 minute. Add the ground chicken and stir-fry until it changes color. Add the bell peppers and stir-fry briefly, then add the Sauce ingredients and basil and combine.
3 Pack the rice into a bento box, top with the stir-fry and egg, and tuck the broccoli on the side (see photo).

Cook the fried egg until the yolk is firm.

VARIATION:

Beef Bowl Bento

Recreate a visit to Japan's popular beef bowl restaurants with this sweet-and-savory dish that's delicious even when cold.

SERVES 1

¼ onion
2 teaspoons vegetable oil
4 oz (120 g) thinly sliced boneless beef short rib
About 1 cup (200 g) cooked rice
Red pickled ginger (beni shoga)

Sauce
2 tablespoons mirin
2 tablespoons water
1 tablespoon soy sauce
1 tablespoon sake

1 Thinly slice the onion.
2 Heat the vegetable oil in a medium skillet and stir-fry the onion over medium heat for about 2 minutes. Add the beef and stir-fry for about 1 minute. Add the Sauce ingredients and simmer until the liquid is reduced by half.
3 Pack a bento box with rice and top with the beef and pickled ginger.

* Does not include calories or cooking times for sides.

Simple Blanched Greens
▶ Page 88

Savory Boiled Eggs
▶ Page 69

Per serving
876
cal

Cooking time
10 min

Kombu and Salmon Rice Ball Bento

Rice balls can be endlessly varied by changing their shape, size and filling. Pairing rice balls wrapped in nori with bright pink rice balls makes for a pretty and colorful bento.

Karaage Fried Chicken
▶ Page 42

Carrots with
Tuna and Eggs
▶ Page 74

Basic Japanese Rolled
Omelet ▶ Page 66

Per serving
410
cal

Cooking time
6 min

* Does not include calories
or cooking time for sides.

SERVES 1

About 1 cup (200 to 240 g)
    cooked rice
Salt
1 tablespoon store-bought
    salmon flakes (sold in jars or
    packets)
Toasted white sesame seeds
2 teaspoons store-bought
    kombu tsukudani preserves
2 strips toasted nori

1 In a small bowl, combine half the rice with the salmon flakes, folding gently to avoid crushing the rice. Form into 2 cylindrical rice balls following the instructions on page 114. Sprinkle with sesame seeds.

2 Divide the remaining rice into 2 portions and stuff each with 1 teaspoon of kombu tsukudani. Form into cylindrical rice balls following the instructions on page 114. Wrap each rice ball with a strip of nori.

Pack in the rice balls tightly into the bento box, starting at one end.

VARIATION:

Smoky Fish and Cod Roe Rice Ball Bento

Rice balls with the filling placed on top instead of inside look great in a bento.

SERVES 1

½ oz (15 g) salted cod roe (tarako),
    about ¼ of a sac
Large pinch bonito flakes
Soy sauce
About 1 cup (180 to 200 g) cooked rice
Salt
2 strips toasted nori

1 Grill or pan-fry the cod roe to cook it through and cut in half. Combine the bonito flakes with a dash of soy sauce. Divide the rice into 3 equal portions.

2 Stuff half the bonito flakes into one portion of rice and form into a cylinder, following the instructions on page 114. Place the rest of the bonito flakes on top of the rice ball.

3 Form the remaining rice into 2 cylinders following the instructions on page 114. Stick a piece of cod roe in the top of each ball. Wrap with nori.

* Does not include calories or cooking time for sides.

Chicken Patties
with Edamame
▶ Page 57

Ham Wrapped
Cherry Tomatoes
▶ Page 76

Miso Marinated Eggs
▶ Page 69

Per serving
341
cal

Cooking time
9 min

How to Make Onigiri Japanese Rice Balls

This is a basic method for making rice balls (onigiri), a staple of Japanese box lunches. Try a triangle, a cylinder or a drum shape—the technique is similar for all three. Alternately, skip the cling wrap and form the balls with damp, lightly salted hands. Be sure to use short or medium grain rice; other varieties aren't sticky enough.

Sprinkle the salt from high above.

1

Spread out a piece of cling film and sprinkle it evenly with salt.

Use about ¼ to ½ cup (60 to 100 g) of cooked rice per rice ball.

2

Place freshly cooked rice in the center of the cling film.

Wrap the rice with cling film.

3

Place filling, if using, in the middle and wrap so the rice surrounds it on all sides

Finished!

Form it into any shape you like.

4

Firmly but gently press the rice into shape. Remove the cling film before wrapping in nori.

Pork-Wrapped Rice Ball with Buttery Corn

1 RICE BALL Combine ⅓ **cup (70 g) warm cooked rice, 2 teaspoons canned whole corn kernels,** and ½ **teaspoon butter**. Form a cylindrical rice ball. Wrap **a thin slice (about 1 oz/30 g) of pork belly** around it and dust with **flour**. Heat vegetable oil in a small skillet and cook the meat through on all sides. Add **yakiniku sauce** and coat the rice ball with it. Optionally wrap with **1 mitsuba stalk**.

Per serving
303 cal

Cooking time
7 min

Miso and Cheese Rice Ball

1 RICE BALL Form ½ **cup (100 g) cooked rice** into a triangular rice ball and place on a lightly oiled piece of aluminum foil. Top the rice ball with ½ **teaspoon miso** and **2 teaspoons shredded pizza cheese**. Bake in a toaster oven until the cheese melts.

Per serving
186 cal

Cooking time
6–7 min

Luncheon Meat Rice Ball

1 RICE BALL Cut **a piece of canned luncheon meat** into a 1¾ x 2⅓ x ⅓ inch (4.5 cm x 6 cm x 8 mm) slice. Pan-fry lightly on both sides. Cut a slice of **rolled omelet** the same size as the luncheon meat. Form ¼ **cup (50–60 g) cooked rice** into a flattish cylindrical rice ball sprinkled lightly with **salt**. Top with omelet, meat and **5 to 6 radish sprouts**. Wrap with a strip of **toasted nori** to secure the toppings.

Per serving
188 cal

Cooking time
4 min

Double Kombu Rice Ball

1 RICE BALL Stuff **1 teaspoon of kombu tsukudani preserves** in ½ **cup (100 g) cooked rice** and form into a cylindrical ball sprinkled lightly with **salt**. Wrap with **oboro kombu** (thinly shaved kombu). Top with more oboro kombu.

Per serving
171 cal

Cooking time
2 min

Karaage Fried Chicken Rice Ball

1 RICE BALL Stick a piece of **Karaage Fried Chicken** (page 42) in the center of ½ **cup (100 g) cooked rice** and form a triangular ball sprinkled lightly with salt. Wrap in toasted nori.

Per serving
249 cal

Cooking time
2 min

Cheese and Smoky Fish Rice Ball

1 RICE BALL Cut ½ **oz (15 g) processed cheese** into ⅓ inch (1 cm) cubes and mix into ½ **cup (100 g) cooked rice**. Form into a triangular rice ball sprinkled lightly with **salt**. Wrap with a strip of toasted nori as shown. Mix **a large pinch of bonito flakes** with **a dash of soy sauce** and place on the rice ball.

Per serving
208 cal

Cooking time
2 min

Sesame Spinach
▶ Page 91

Per serving
671
cal

Cooking time
8 min

Fried Rice Bento

Well-flavored, fragrant fried rice is a great bento main.
This hearty recipe includes pork belly as well as shrimp.

* Does not include
calories or cooking
time for the side.

SERVES 1

1 oz (30 g) thinly sliced pork belly
½ teaspoon sake
½ teaspoon soy sauce
1 tablespoon sesame oil
One 4-inch (10-cm) piece green
  onion
2 oz (50 g) small peeled shrimp
7 oz (200 g) cooked rice
1 teaspoon granulated chicken
  bouillon
1 teaspoon soy sauce
1 egg
Salt and pepper

1 Cut the pork into thin strips, and sprinkle with ½ teaspoon each of sake and soy sauce. Mince the green onion.
2 Heat the sesame oil in a medium skillet and stir-fry the pork for about 1 minute over medium heat. When the meat changes color, add the shrimp and green onion and stir-fry for another minute.
3 When the shrimp are cooked through, add the rice and granulated bouillon and stir-fry briefly. Drizzle in the soy sauce. Push the rice to one side and crack the egg on the empty side of the skillet. Mix to scramble. When cooked, mix with the rice and season with salt and pepper.

Leave space for the side dish.

VARIATION:

Curry Pilaf Bento
Bell pepper and corn kernels brighten up this tasty curry–flavored rice.

SERVES 1

2 teaspoons olive oil
⅙ onion, minced
1 oz (20 g) canned corned beef
1 small green bell pepper, minced
2 tablespoons canned or frozen corn kernels
1 cup (200 g) cooked rice
1 teaspoon granulated chicken bouillon
1 teaspoon soy sauce
½ tablespoon curry powder
Salt and pepper

1 Heat the olive oil in a skillet and stir-fry the onion and corned beef for 1 to 2 minutes.
2 When the onion has softened and the corned beef is flaky, add the bell pepper and corn and stir-fry briefly. Add the rice, granulated bouillon, soy sauce and curry. Season with salt and pepper.

* Does not include calories or cooking time for the sides.

Baked Asparagus
with Peppery Cheese
▶ Page 87

Honey Lemon
Cherry Tomatoes
▶ Page 76

Per serving
489
cal

Cooking time
7 min

Tuna & Mushroom Rice Bento

This is a type of *takikomi gohan*, a Japanese dish of rice cooked with vegetables, meat or seafood and seasonings. Since a rice cooker does all the cooking, it's a great time-saver. You can wrap the cooked rice in individual portions and freeze for up to a month. Substitute other kinds of mushrooms if the Japanese varieties are not available.

Pan-fried salmon

Cherry tomatoes

Spicy Eggplant Wedges
▶ Page 94

Per serving
348
cal

Cooking time
5 min

* Does not include calories or cooking time for the sides or cooking time for the rice.

4 SERVINGS

1½ cups (300 g) uncooked short grain rice
4 oz (100 g) shimeji mushrooms
4 oz (100 g) maitake mushrooms
2 tablespoons light soy sauce
1 tablespoon sake
1 tablespoon mirin
Water
3 oz (80 g) canned tuna
2 teaspoons butter
Coarsely ground black pepper

1 Rinse the rice and drain in a colander. Cut the stem ends off the mushrooms and divide into small clumps. Drain the tuna.
2 Place the drained rice, soy sauce, sake and mirin in a rice cooker and add water to just below the 2-cup mark. Add the tuna, mushrooms and butter and cook in the rice cooker.
3 When the rice is done, mix gently and sprinkle with the black pepper.

Arrange the mushrooms on top of the rice in the bento box.

VARIATION:

Chicken & Sweet Potato Rice Bento

The sweet potato provide a nice flavor and texture accent. Try to find Japanese sweet potatoes, which are drier than Western varieties.

4 SERVINGS

1½ cups (300 g) uncooked short grain rice
Water
4 oz (120 g) boneless chicken breast
7 oz (200 g) sweet potato

Marinade
½ tablespoon light soy sauce
1 tablespoon sake
2 tablespoons mirin
2 teaspoons dashi stock granules

1 Rinse the rice and drain in a colander. Cut the chicken into small pieces. Combine the Marinade ingredients and marinate the chicken for about 10 minutes. Cut the sweet potato into bite-size pieces and soak in a bowl of water.
2 Put the drained rice and chicken marinade in a rice cooker and add water to just below the 2-cup mark. Add the chicken and drained sweet potato and cook in the rice cooker.

* Does not include calories or cooking time for the sides or cooking time for the rice.

Rolled omelet with crunchy pickled plum

Boiled green beans

Toasted black sesame seeds

Microwave Simmered Vegetables ▶ Page 93

Per serving
388 cal

Cooking time
15 min

Cucumber and Cottage
Cheese Salad
▶ Page 89

Boiled quail egg

Per serving
366
cal

Cooking time
3 min

Rice with Roasted Pork and Bamboo Shoot Bento

Folding flavorful ingredients like lacto-fermented bamboo shoots (menma) and Chinese-style roast pork (char siu) into steamed rice is another easy way to make rice the centerpiece of your bento.

* Does not include calories or cooking time for sides or cooking time for the rice.

SERVES 1

1 cup (200 g) cooked rice
1 oz (30 g) store-bought fermented bamboo shoots (menma) or canned bamboo shoots
1 oz (30 g) store-bought Chinese style roast pork (char siu)
A few leaves of mitsuba or flat-leaf parsley

1 Chop the pork roughly and heat in the microwave for 20 to 30 seconds. Chop the bamboo shoots and mitsuba or parsley leaves roughly.
2 Add the pork, bamboo shoots, and mitsuba or parsley to the cooked rice and mix well.

TIP: Warming the pork in the microwave helps its flavor permeate the rice.

VARIATION:

Rice with Tiny Fish Bento

This recipe calls for chirimen jako, dried baby sardines available in Japanese grocery stores. The leftover Seasoned Tiny Fish can be used to top rice later in the week.

SERVES 1

1 cup (200 g) cooked rice

Seasoned Tiny Fish
1 teaspoon sesame oil
1 oz (30 g) dried baby anchovies (chirimen jako)
1½ tablespoons sake
1½ tablespoons mirin
2 teaspoons soy sauce
2 teaspoons sugar
1 tablespoon toasted white sesame seeds

1 To make the Seasoned Tiny Fish, heat the sesame oil in a skillet and stir-fry the dried anchovies for about 1 minute. Add the sake, mirin, soy sauce and sugar and mix to coat. Add the sesame seeds and mix.
2 Add ¼ to ⅓ of the Seasoned Tiny Fish to the rice and fold in gently.

* Does not include calories or cooking time for the sides or cooking time for the rice.
* Storage time is for the Seasoned Tiny Fish.

Boiled broccoli

Bell Pepper with Honey Mustard
▶ Page 77

Salted pan-fried mackerel

Per serving	Cooking time		Keeps in the fridge for
377 cal	**5** min	Make-Ahead	**5** days

Six Great Rice Toppings

Here are just a few ideas for "rice companions" to perk up the classic bento carb. All of these toppings can be bought pre-made at a Japanese grocery store.

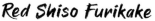

Salmon Flakes

Arrange in a ring on top of the rice.

Red Shiso Furikake

Make a cross pattern.

Kombu Seaweed Tsukudani

Simply place in the center of the rice!

Steamed Rice

If using a rice cooker, wash, soak and drain the rice as described in steps 1 and 2 before transferring to the rice cooker pot and cooking according to product instructions.

MAKES ABOUT 2.5 CUPS (500 G)

1 cup (200 g) uncooked short grain rice
1 cup (240 ml) water

1 In a medium bowl, wash the rice in several changes of water and drain.
2 Cover rice with water and soak for about 30 minutes. Drain in a fine sieve.
3 Place the drained rice in a pot and add the water. Bring to a boil over high heat, turn the heat down to low, cover and cook for 12 minutes. Remove from heat and let steam with the lid on for 10 minutes.
4 Fluff the rice gently with a moistened wooden paddle before packing into bento boxes.

Bonito Flakes + Toasted Nori

Mix the bonito flakes with a dash of soy sauce before scattering over the rice.

Salted Cod Roe

Grill or pan-fry the salted cod roe (*tarako*), cut in chunks, and nestle on one side of the rice.

Crunchy Pickled Plums

Chop the crunchy pickled plums (kari kari ume), removing any seeds, and scatter over the rice.

Egg Salad & Vegetable Sandwiches

Sandwiches are great when you don't have a lot of time to eat your lunch. This one features bright, crunchy carrot and cucumber along with egg salad.

Per serving
488
cal

* Does not include boiling time for the egg.

Cooking time
10 min

SERVES 1

3-inch (7-cm) piece carrot
Salt
2 teaspoons rice vinegar
2 teaspoons sugar
¼ small cucumber
1 boiled egg, peeled
1½ tablespoons mayonnaise
2 slices sandwich bread
1 teaspoon butter, softened

1 Shred the carrot and massage with a pinch of salt. Mix with the vinegar and sugar. Cut the cucumber into thin diagonal slices. Chop the boiled egg and mix with the mayonnaise.

2 Butter the bread on one side and layer with the egg salad, carrot and cucumber. Wrap with cling film or wax paper, leave to rest for about 5 minutes, and cut in halves or quarters.

Sandwich Basics

You can use wax paper instead of cling film.

1

Butter the bread and place in the center of the cling film.

Spread the filling to the corners of the bread.

2

Layer on the fillings.

Line up the bread slices facing the same direction.

3

Butter the other slice of bread and place on top.

Let the bread and fillings meld together.

4

Finished!

Wrap with cling film.

TIP: For preschoolers, cut off the crusts.

Check the height of the bento box so you know how wide to cut the pieces.

When slicing the sandwich, cut with the cling film on.

Per serving
536 cal

Cooking time
15 min *

BLTE Sandwich

An attractive tri-color sandwich that adds a fried egg to the classic BLT.

SERVES 1

1 teaspoon vegetable oil
1 egg
2 slices bacon
2 slices sandwich bread
1 teaspoon butter, softened
1 lettuce leaf
1 thick slice tomato

1 Heat the vegetable oil in a medium skillet, break in the egg and cook in the middle of the pan for about 3 minutes. Meanwhile, cook the bacon on either side of the egg for 2 to 3 minutes on each side. After 3 minutes, reduce heat to low and cook the egg for another 3 minutes (see photo).
2 Butter one slice of the bread and layer with the lettuce, tomato, bacon and fried egg. Top with the other buttered slice of bread. Wrap with cling film or wax paper, leave for about 5 minutes to settle, and cut into halves or quarters.

Fry the egg until the yolk is firm.

Per serving
535 cal

Cooking time
15 min*

Fried Ham Cutlet Sandwich

This hearty sandwich features a fried cutlet made with 4 layered slices of ham.

SERVES 1

4 slices ham
2 tablespoons flour
2 tablespoons water
Panko breadcrumbs
Tonkatsu sauce
2 slices sandwich bread
1 teaspoon butter, softened
1 teaspoon French mustard
1 oz (30 g) shredded cabbage
Vegetable oil for frying

1 Stack the ham slices. Combine the flour and water. Coat the ham with this paste and then the breadcrumbs.
2 Heat about ¾ inch (2 cm) of vegetable oil in a small skillet to 355 °F (180 °C; see Tip page 42) and fry the ham cutlet until golden brown, about 3 minutes (see photo). Top with tonkatsu sauce.
3 Butter the bread and spread with French mustard. Layer on the ham cutlet and shredded cabbage. Wrap with cling film or wax paper, leave to settle for 5 minutes, and cut into halves or quarters.

Drain the oil well after frying the cutlet.

Chicken & Potato Salad Bagelwich

The chicken, potato salad, and chewy bagel make for a very satisfying sandwich.

SERVES 1

1 bagel
1 teaspoon butter, softened
Potato Salad (page 99)
Steamed Chicken (see recipe below), shredded
1 lettuce leaf

1 Cut the bagel in half, spread with butter, and layer with lettuce, potato salad and chicken.

STEAMED CHICKEN

Season **2 oz (50 g) boneless chicken breast** with **salt** (use herbed salt if you have it), **black pepper** and **1 teaspoon sake**. Rub in the seasonings. Wrap in cling film and microwave for 1 to 2 minutes.

Per serving
401 cal

Cooking time
3 min

* Does not include cooking time for the Steamed Chicken or Potato Salad. You can substitute store-bought cooked chicken and potato salad.

Cocktail Frank & Croquette Rolls

It's fun to have two different mini sandwiches for lunch, and since the fillings for both are easy to prepare, it only takes a few minutes.

SERVES 1

2 small rolls
1 teaspoon mayonnaise
1 cocktail frank
1 piece lettuce
½ store-bought croquette
3 diagonal slices cucumber
French mustard
Tonkatsu sauce

1 Slice open the rolls and spread with mayonnaise. Cut evenly spaced slits in the cocktail frank and cook briefly in a small skillet over medium heat.
2 Stuff one role with the lettuce and cocktail frank and the other with the cucumber and croquette. Top the cocktail frank with mustard and the croquette with tonkatsu sauce.

Per serving
514 cal

Cooking time
4 min

Sloppy Joe Dog

Hot dog buns work well in place of the traditional hamburger bun in this sandwich.

SERVES 1

⅛ **onion**
¼ **tomato**
1 teaspoon vegetable oil
2 oz (60 g) ground beef
1 tablespoon frozen mixed vegetables
Salt and pepper
1 hot dog bun

Sauce
1 tablespoon ketchup
½ tablespoon curry powder
½ tablespoon chuno sauce
A little hot sauce
Lettuce

1 Chop the onion and cut the tomato into small cubes.
2 Heat the vegetable oil in a small skillet and add the ground beef. Stir-fry until crumbly. Add the mixed vegetables and tomato and stir-fry for about 1 minute. Add the Sauce ingredients and simmer to reduce slightly. Season with salt and pepper.
3 Line the bun with lettuce and stuff with filling.

Per serving
389
cal

Cooking time
8 min

Chicken Teriyaki & Egg Baguette

Sweet and savory Chicken Teriyaki makes a delicious sandwich filling.

SERVES 1

4–5 inch (10–12 cm) piece baguette
1 teaspoon mayonnaise
½ hard boiled egg
3 to 4 slices Chicken Teriyaki (page 40)
1 piece curly lettuce

1 Cut 2 lengthwise slits in the baguette and toast in a toaster oven for 30 to 40 seconds. Spread mayonnaise in each slit. Slice the boiled egg.
2 Stuff the lettuce and chicken teriyaki in one slit and the boiled egg in the other.

Per serving
564
cal

Cooking time
3 min

* Does not include cooking time for the Chicken Teriyaki or boiled egg.

Per serving
635 cal

Cooking time
15 min

Chilled Noodle Bento

Refreshing chilled noodles topped with vegetables, chicken and egg are welcome in summer. This colorful and appetizing version features 6 different toppings.

SERVES 1

1 hank fresh ramen or Chinese egg noodles
  (about 5 oz/150 g)
Sesame oil
2 chicken tenders (4 oz/100 g)
Salt and pepper
2 teaspoons sake
3 cherry tomatoes
¼ small cucumber
1 hardboiled egg, peeled
2 tablespoons shelled boiled edamame
3 tablespoons canned or frozen corn kernels

Sauce
1½ tablespoons soy sauce
2 teaspoons rice vinegar
2 teaspoons sugar
1 teaspoon sesame oil
1 teaspoon toasted sesame seeds

1 Boil the noodles following package instructions. Drain and cool in cold water. Drain well again, drizzle with sesame oil, and pack into a bento box.

2 Remove the tendons from the chicken tenders and place in a heatproof container. Season with the salt, pepper and sake, cover with cling film and microwave for 2 minutes. Shred when cool. Cut the cherry tomatoes in half and the cucumber in thin strips. Slice the boiled egg.

3 Top the noodles with the tomato, cucumber, egg, chicken edamame and corn.

4 Combine the Sauce ingredients in a separate small container. Pour the sauce over the noodles and toppings just before eating.

Pre-made sauce (sold as "hiyashi chuka sauce") may be available at Japanese groceries.

VARIATION:

Chilled Somen Bento

Separating the noodles into small bundles is key to making this bento easy to eat.

SERVES 1

½ cup (125 ml) mentsuyu (not concentrated)
Several ice cubes
4 oz (100 g) dried somen noodles (1 bundle)
1 okra
2 large shrimp, peeled and deveined
1 small Asian eggplant
1 teaspoon vegetable oil
Red shiso furikake

Per serving **469** cal   Cooking time **15** min

1 Put the mentsuyu and ice cubes in a small thermos.
2 Boil the somen noodles for 1 to 2 minutes. Drain and cool in cold water. Drain again and divide into small portions. Wrap each portion into a spiral and put in a bento box.
3 Boil the shrimp for about 1 minute. Rub the okra firmly on a cutting board to eliminate the surface hairs, boil briefly and slice into rounds.
4 Cut the eggplant into 4 pieces and place on a heatproof plate. Sprinkle with the vegetable oil, cover with cling film and microwave for 1 to 2 minutes, until softened.
5 Top the noodles with the shrimp, okra, eggplant and furikake (see photo) and tuck the eggplant in on the side. Eat with sauce.

Boiled edamame

Noodles with Miso Dipping Sauce Bento

Warm noodles are a comforting bento for fall and winter. Pack a piping hot sauce in a separate small thermos to ensure the noodles stay firm and delicious until lunchtime.

Per serving
904
cal

Cooking time
15 min

SERVES 1

1 hank fresh ramen or Chinese egg
noodles (about 5 oz/150 g)
Sesame oil
2 oz (50 g) spinach
4 oz (100 g) thinly sliced pork belly
Salt and pepper
½ hard boiled egg
Toasted sesame seeds
Minced green onion

Sauce
1 tablespoon miso
1 tablespoon concentrated mentsuyu
1 tablespoon oyster sauce
½ teaspoon granulated chicken
bouillon
Chili sesame oil (rayu)
Black pepper
1¼ cups (300 ml) water

1 Combine the Sauce ingredients in a small saucepan and bring to a boil over medium heat. Pour into a thermos.
2 Boil the noodles for 40 to 50 seconds less than the time indicated on the package. Drain well and drizzle with a little sesame oil. Boil the spinach for about 1 minute, drain thoroughly and cut into 1-inch (3-cm) pieces.
3 Season the pork with salt and pepper and cut into bite-size pieces. Heat a medium skillet and cook the pork over medium heat for about 2 minutes.
4 Pack the noodles, egg, pork, and spinach into a bento box. Top the spinach with sesame seeds and the noodles with green onion.

Instead of cooking the sauce in a pan, you can put the ingredients in a heatproof measuring cup, mix and microwave 4 to 5 minutes.

* After the sauce is heated, wait for the bubbles to subside before pouring into the thermos.

VARIATION:

Udon with Hearty Soup Bento
Before eating, pour a little of the broth over the noodles to loosen. Use the rest for dipping.

SERVES 1

One 4-inch (10-cm) piece fat
green onion
2 oz (60 g) thinly sliced pork
½ piece aburaage (fried tofu)
1 packet frozen or fresh udon
noodles

1 teaspoon minced
green onion

Broth
2 tablespoon store-bought
shirodashi
1 teaspoon mirin
1 teaspoon soy sauce
1¼ cups (300 ml) water

Chicken with Japanese
Root Vegetables
▶ Page 96

1 Cut the piece of green onion into thin diagonal slices.
2 Put the Broth ingredients in a pan and bring to a boil. Add the pork, sliced green onion and aburaage and simmer for 2 to 3 minutes over medium heat. Skim off any scum. When the ingredients are cooked through, pack the sauce in a thermos.
3 Wet the udon noodles quickly under running water and microwave for about 2 minutes (or follow package directions for frozen udon noodles) to warm them up. Transfer to a colander and rinse under cold running water. Drain well, pack into a bento box and top with the minced green onion.

*To keep the soup hot for longer, pre-warm the thermos by filling it with boiling water and draining before pouring in the soup.

Per serving
422 cal

Cooking time
15 min

Spaghetti Napolitan Bento

Spaghetti Napolitan is a classic Japanese pasta dish. It works well in a bento because the pasta doesn't suffer from being mixed with the sauce ahead of time. Plus, it includes enough veggies and protein to serve as a main dish.

Cherry
tomatoes

Ham and Cheese
Spirals
▶ Page 104

Cauliflower with
Cottage Cheese
▶ Page 99

Per serving
731
cal

Cooking time
15 min

* Does not include calories and cooking
time for sides.

SERVES 1

4 oz (100 g) quick-cooking
  spaghetti
Olive oil
¼ onion
1 king oyster mushroom
1 small green bell pepper
1-inch (2-cm) piece carrot
2 cocktail franks
2 teaspoons vegetable oil
3 tablespoons ketchup
1 tablespoon chuno sauce
Salt and pepper
Grated Parmesan

1 Boil the spaghetti following the package instructions, adding a splash of olive oil to the cooking water. Thinly slice the onion and king oyster mushroom. Seed the bell pepper and slice thinly. Cut the carrot into thin strips. Cut the franks into thin diagonal slices.
2 Heat the vegetable oil in a medium skillet and stir-fry the onion and carrot for about 1 minute. When they are softened, add the cocktail franks, bell pepper and mushroom and stir-fry for 1 to 2 minutes.
3 Add the drained spaghetti, ketchup and chuno sauce, and stir fry until excess moisture has evaporated. Season with salt and pepper and sprinkle with Parmesan.

> **TIP:** Adding olive oil to the water for boiling the spaghetti keeps the noodles from sticking together.

VARIATION:

Penne Carbonara Bento
Penne is an easy pasta shape for kids to eat.
Cream, bacon and butter make this a rich dish.

SERVES 1

3 oz (80 g) quick-cooking penne
Olive oil
¼ onion
1 slice bacon
2 teaspoons butter
3 tablespoons heavy cream
½ tablespoon grated Parmesan
1 egg yolk
Salt and coarsely ground black pepper
Dried parsley

1 Boil the penne following package instructions, adding a splash of olive oil to the cooking water. Thinly slice the onion and cut the bacon into ⅓ inch (1 cm) strips.
2 Heat the butter in a skillet and stir-fry the onion for about 1 minute. When it is softened add the bacon and stir-fry till cooked through.
3 Add the cream and penne and stir to combine. Stir in the Parmesan and egg yolk and continue to cook, stirring, for 20 to 30 seconds to cook the egg through. Season with salt and pepper and sprinkle with dried parsley.

Per serving
750 cal

Cooking time
15 min

Yakisoba Bento

Yakisoba is another popular Japanese noodle dish that works great in a bento. This version features lightly seasoned stir-fried noodles and loads of colorful vegetables. Pre-cooked yakisoba noodles are sold in individual portions in the refrigerated section of Japanese grocery stores. If you use fresh Chinese egg noodles, boil them al dente before adding to the stir-fry.

Baby Corn and Cheese
▶ Page 83

Per serving
669
cal

Cooking time
15 min

* Does not include calories and cooking time for the side.

SERVES 1

2 oz (60 g) komatsuna greens or Swiss chard
1-inch (2-cm) piece carrot
4-inch (10-cm) piece fat green onion
2 oz (60 g) thinly sliced pork belly
Salt and coarsely ground black pepper
2 teaspoons vegetable oil
1 egg
1 packet fresh yakisoba or hank Chinese egg noodles, pre-cooked (about 5 oz/150 g)
1 teaspoon granulated chicken bouillon
2 tablespoons water

1 Cut the komatsuna greens or chard into 1-inch (3-cm) strips. Cut the carrot into thin strips. Cut the green onion into thin diagonal slices. Season the pork with salt and pepper and cut into 1-inch (3-cm) wide pieces.

2 Heat the vegetable oil in a medium skillet, break in the egg and fry over medium heat for 3 minutes. Turn the heat down to low and cook for another 3 to 4 minutes. Remove from the skillet.

3 Heat the skillet again and stir-fry the greens, carrot, green onion and pork for about 2 minutes. Add the noodles, granulated bouillon and water and loosen up the noodles. Cover with a lid and steam for about 1 minute. Remove the lid and stir-fry until the moisture has evaporated. Season with salt and pepper and pack into a bento box.

4 Top the noodles with the fried egg and sprinkle with salt and coarsely ground black pepper.

TIP: Be sure to cook the fried egg thoroughly to prevent spoilage.

VARIATION:

Omelet–Wrapped Yakisoba Bento

This more heavily seasoned variation is tucked inside a paper–thin omelet.

SERVES 1

1 cabbage leaf (2 oz/50 g)
⅛ onion
2 oz (60 g) thinly sliced pork
2 teaspoons vegetable oil
1 packet yakisoba or hank Chinese egg noodles, pre-cooked (about 5 oz/150 g)

2 tablespoons water
2 tablespoons chuno sauce
Salt and pepper
1 egg
A pinch of salt
Tonkatsu sauce
Aonori powder
Red pickled ginger (beni shoga)

Spicy Lotus Root
▶ Page 98

1 Roughly chop the cabbage. Thinly slice the onion. Cut the pork into bite-size pieces.

2 Heat the vegetable oil in a medium skillet and stir-fry the cabbage, onion and pork for 1 to 2 minutes. Add the noodles and water and stir-fry until the moisture evaporates. Add the chuno sauce and mix. Season with salt and pepper and pack in a bento box.

3 Wipe out the pan and add a little vegetable oil. Beat the egg and salt and pour into the pan. Cook over low heat until the surface has dried out. Flip and cook the other side. Drape over the noodles and tuck in the sides.

4 Top with tonkatsu sauce, aonori powder and beni shoga.

* Does not include calories and cooking time for the side.

Per serving
610 cal

Cooking time
10 min

Lesson

\ Attractive bentos without the fuss! /

Picnic Bentos

The Japanese tradition of packing a special picnic bento for sports events and outdoor festivities like cherry blossom viewing can be exhausting for the cook. Check out these tips for making easy but impressive bentos for a crowd.

Main 1

Beef and Cheese Rolls
▶ Page 54

`Brown`

Main 2

Gingery Fried Salmon
▶ Page 63

`Brown`

Starch

Sushi-Roll-Style Rice Balls
▶ Page 139

`White` `Green`

`Red` `Black`

`Yellow`

Side

Basic Japanese Rolled Omelet
▶ Page 66

`Yellow`

Secondary Side 1

Glazed Sweet Potato Chunks
▶ Page 85

`Yellow`

`Make-Ahead`

Secondary Side 2

Sesame-Miso Green Beans
▶ Page 86

`Green`

Cooking time
35 min

Approximate Bento Box Size		
For 4 to 6 people	4 cups (1000 ml)	Amount of rice: 2 cups (450g)

Picnic Bento Rules

Prep the day before by marinating and breading ingredients

Classic picnic bentos typically have a lot of dishes, so the cook is very busy on the morning of the event. Do as much advance prep as possible by pre-seasoning and breading ingredients the day before.

Make food that is easy to hand out and eat

Choose mostly foods that can be picked up with your hands so they are easier to distribute. I also recommend foods skewered with picks.

Use sides to add color

If you choose brown mains like fried foods, add green, red and yellow sides and secondary sides and colorful starches for visual balance.

Make a drawing of how you'll pack the food

When packing a large bento box with several dishes, things go much more smoothly if you plan out the arrangement in advance and even draw a diagram for yourself.

Timing Guide

Get foods marinating and coated right away.

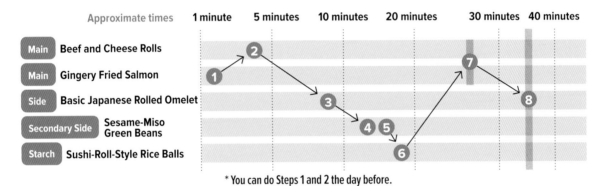

Approximate times	1 minute	5 minutes	10 minutes	20 minutes	30 minutes	40 minutes
Main Beef and Cheese Rolls		②				
Main Gingery Fried Salmon	①				⑦	
Side Basic Japanese Rolled Omelet			③			⑧
Secondary Side Sesame-Miso Green Beans				④ ⑤		
Starch Sushi-Roll-Style Rice Balls				⑥		

* You can do Steps 1 and 2 the day before.

① Marinate the salmon.

② Bread the beef cutlets.

③ Make the rolled omelet and let cool.

④ Bring a small pan of water to a boil and cook the green beans for the side and rice balls.

⑤ Make the Sesame-Miso Green Beans.

⑥ Make the Sushi-Roll-Style Rice Balls.

⑦ Heat the vegetable oil and deep-fry the Gingery Fried Salmon and Beef and Cheese Rolls.

⑧ Let the food cool while you clean up. When everything is cool, pack into bento boxes.

Sushi-Roll-Style Rice Balls　　SERVES 4 TO 6

Place **half a sheet of toasted nori** on a sheet of cling film and sprinkle with salt. Spread **¾ cup (150 g) cooked rice** over it. Put **two 4-inch (10-cm) sticks of takuan pickle** and **2 salted boiled green beans** in the center. Roll up from one end. Make a similar roll with **two 4-inch (10-cm) strips of char siu roast pork** and **one 4-inch (10-cm) stick of cucumber**. Make another of these. Wrap each roll in cling film and form into triangular bars. Leave for a minute to settle, then cut into 1-inch (2.5-cm) slices.

Glossary of Japanese Ingredients

Most of the ingredients listed below are available online, at Japanese grocery stores, and increasingly at large conventional groceries. Recipes for homemade versions of the sauces are widely available online.

Aburaage are thin, golden brown sheets of deep-fried tofu.

Atsuage are thicker cutlets of deep-fried tofu.

Bonito flakes (*katsuobushi*) give dashi and many other Japanese dishes a smoky, umami-rich flavor. Shaved from aged bonito, the flakes are used in this book as a garnish and seasoning.

Chirimen jako are tiny dried anchovies, sardines and herring used as a topping for rice and other foods.

Chuno sauce is similar to Worcestershire sauce, but thicker and less acidic. Can be used as a substitute for yakisoba sauce or tonkatsu sauce. In a pinch, substitute ketchup mixed with Worcestershire sauce and a little honey.

Doubanjiang is a spicy, fermented Chinese bean paste sometimes labeled "toban djan."

Gochujang is a Korean spicy bean paste.

Fishcakes come in many shapes and colors, including tube-shaped **chikuwa**, spongy white **hanpen**, and deep-fried **satsumaage**.

Furikake is a dry mixed seasoning, often including nori flakes, that is sprinkled on cooked rice. Popular flavors include red shiso, salmon, and wasabi.

Kiriboshi daikon is thin strips of dried daikon radish that is often simmered to make a side dish.

Mentsuyu is a seasoning made from sake, mirin, soy sauce, kombu, and bonito flakes. It is used as a broth or dipping sauce for noodles and is also a handy seasoning for other dishes. Pre-made varieties are sold in a range of concentrations for diluting or using straight from the bottle. It's easy to make at home, too.

Oboro kombu is thinly shaved kombu with a light, soft texture and umami-rich flavor.

Ponzu sauce is a citrusy, savory sauce traditionally made with fragrant yuzu juice. Commercial versions are widely available, and it's also easy to make at home.

Pickled plums (*umeboshi*) are intensely sour, salty pickles that are a classic topping for steamed rice, especially in bentos. A related pickle called *kari kari ume* is crunchy, in contrast to the soft texture of *umeboshi*.

Shio kombu is kombu flavored with soy sauce and other seasonings. The intensely flavored strips can be used to top rice or as an ingredient in salads and quick pickles.

Shirodashi is an intensely flavored seasoning made from dashi, soy sauce, and other ingredients. Having a bottle in the fridge is an easy way to add a burst of complex flavor to vegetables and broths.

Salted Cod Roe (*tarako*) is sold in its sac either frozen or refrigerated.

Spicy Cod Roe (*mentaiko*) is a spicy version of the salted roe.

Takuan is a strongly flavored type of pickled daikon radish. Commercial brands are often bright yellow; traditional versions are cream or tan.

Thinly sliced meat is called for in many recipes in this book. Look for it at Asian groceries, ask your butcher to slice it for you, or slice blocks of meat yourself. Partially freezing the meat and using a very sharp knife makes the job easier.

Tonkatsu sauce is a thick, sweet and tangy sauce served with breaded pork cutlets and other fried foods. It can be used as a substitute for chuno sauce and yakisoba sauce.

Tsukudani are salty preserves made by cooking ingredients in soy sauce and sugar or mirin. This cookbook recommends kombu tsukudani as a topping for rice or a filling for rice balls.

Index

"Books to Span the East and West"

Tuttle Publishing was founded in 1832 in the small New England town of Rutland, Vermont [USA]. Our core values remain as strong today as they were then—to publish best-in-class books which bring people together one page at a time. In 1948, we established a publishing outpost in Japan—and Tuttle is now a leader in publishing English-language books about the arts, languages and cultures of Asia. The world has become a much smaller place today and Asia's economic and cultural influence has grown. Yet the need for meaningful dialogue and information about this diverse region has never been greater. Over the past seven decades, Tuttle has published thousands of books on subjects ranging from martial arts and paper crafts to language learning and literature—and our talented authors, illustrators, designers and photographers have won many prestigious awards. We welcome you to explore the wealth of information available on Asia at www.tuttlepublishing.com.

Published by Tuttle Publishing, an imprint of Periplus Editions (HK) Ltd.

www.tuttlepublishing.com

ISBN: 978-4-8053-1819-5

© Sachiko Horie / Gakken
First published in Japan 2022 by Gakken Plus Co. Ltd., Tokyo
English translation rights arranged with Gakken Inc.
through Japan UNI Agency, Inc., Tokyo

English translation © 2024 Periplus Editions (HK) Ltd.
Translated from the Japanese by Makiko Itoh

Original Japanese edition creative staff
Photography Misa Nakagaki | **Design** Moe Hirota (Bunkyo Zuan-shitsu) | **Styling** Yukiko Hongo | **Cooking Assistant** Yoko Inoue | **Editing and Layout** Miki Maruyama (SORA Kikaku) | **Editorial Assistant** Chihiro Kakimoto (SORA Kikaku) **Calorie Calculations** Sae Fujii | **Proof Reading** Zero Mega

27 26 25 24   10 9 8 7 6 5 4 3 2 1
Printed in China   2406EP

Distributed by

North America, Latin America & Europe
Tuttle Publishing
364 Innovation Drive
North Clarendon, VT 05759-9436 U.S.A.
Tel: 1 (802) 773 8930
Fax: 1 (802) 773 6993
info@tuttlepublishing.com
www.tuttlepublishing.com

Japan
Tuttle Publishing
Yaekari Building 3rd Floor
5-4-12 Osaki
Shinagawa-ku
Tokyo 141-0032
Tel: (81) 3 5437 0171
Fax: (81) 3 5437 0755
sales@tuttle.co.jp
www.tuttle.co.jp

Asia Pacific
Berkeley Books Pte. Ltd.
3 Kallang Sector #04-01
Singapore 349278
Tel: (65) 6741 2178
Fax: (65) 6741 2179
inquiries@periplus.com.sg
www.tuttlepublishing.com